Global
Childhoods

 Monica Edwards

Series Editor Chelle Davison

CRITICAL APPROACHES TO THE EARLY YEARS

First published in 2015 by Critical Publishing Ltd
Reprinted in 2017

British Library Cataloguing in Publication Data
A CIP record for this book is available from the British Library

ISBN: 978-1-909682-69-6

This book is also available in the following e-book formats:

MOBI: 978-1-909682-70-2
EPUB: 978-1-909682-71-9
Adobe e-book reader: 978-1-909682-72-6

Cover and text design by Greensplash Limited
Project Management by Out of House Publishing
Typeset by Newgen Knowledge Works
Printed and bound in Great Britain by 4edge Limited

Critical Publishing
3 Connaught Road
St Albans
AL3 5RX
www.criticalpublishing.com

Paper from responsible sources

Contents

Meet the series editor and author

Chelle Davison is Head of Department, Undergraduate Initial Teacher Education, in the Faculty of Education, Arts and Business at the University of Cumbria. The department has over 450 trainees studying early years, primary, secondary and SEN initial teacher education. Chelle has made significant contributions to a range of policy documents and government reviews, and is a devoted supporter of the professionalisation of the early years workforce.

Monica Edwards is a senior lecturer at Manchester Metropolitan University teaching on the early years and childhood studies undergraduate programme. She has worked with children, adults and families from a wide range of cultural and social backgrounds in the fields of health and education for over 30 years.

Preface: introduction to critical thinking

What is critical thinking?

This section gives you the opportunity to learn more about critical thinking and the skills you will acquire as you use this series. It will introduce you to the meaning of critical thinking and how you can develop the necessary skills to read and research effectively towards a critical approach to learning and analysis. It is a necessary and wholly beneficial position to be starting with questions and finishing your journey with more questions.

> *Judge a man by his questions rather than by his answers.*
>
> François-Marie Arouet (Voltaire)

If you are already a professional within the early years sector, maybe as a teacher in a Reception class, or maybe as an early years educator in a private daycare setting, you will no doubt have faced many challenging debates, discussions at training events and your own personal questioning of the policies faced by the sector as a whole. We want you to ask these questions. More importantly we believe it to be an essential and crucial part of your professional development. You will no doubt be required to implement the policies that might at first seem detached from your day-to-day teaching and practice. It is critical that you question these policies, that you understand their purpose and moreover that you understand how they have come into being. Often students are faced with complex definitions of critical thinking that require them to deconstruct the concept before they fully understand just how to *do* the critical thinking in the first place. For example,

> *Critical thinking is the intellectually disciplined process of actively and skilfully conceptualizing, applying, analysing, synthesizing, and/or evaluating information gathered from, or generated by, observation, experience, reflection, reasoning, or communication, as a guide to belief and action.*
>
> (Scriven and Paul, 1989)

Rather than confusing you with expressive academic definitions, it is our hope that as you read further and begin to understand this topic more, you will be encouraged to ask contemplative questions. Alison King emphasises the importance of students acquiring and cultivating 'a habit of inquiry' (1995, p 13) to enable them to 'learn to ask thoughtful questions' (King, 1995). Contrary to the standard methods of instruction that leave the students as passive recipients of information, King argues that where the students have developed the skills of critical thinking, they become autonomous learners:

> Such a habit of inquiry learned and practiced in class can be applied also to their everyday lives: to what they see on television, read in the newspaper, observe in popular culture and hear during interaction with friends and colleagues, as well as to decisions they make about personal relationships, consumer purchases, political choices, and business transactions.
>
> (King, 1995, p 13)

Consider the subject matter that you are now researching; you may have been tasked with the question, 'How has policy changed over the past 25 years?'. This is what King would suggest is a factual question, one that may well have a limited answer. Once you have this answer, there is a tendency to stop there, making the inquiry fact-based rather than critical. If you were to follow-up this first question with a critical question, King would argue that you are beginning to 'introduce high level cognitive processes such as analysis of ideas, comparison and contrast, inference, prediction [and] evaluation' (1995, p 140).

Example:

Factual question	Critical question
How has policy changed over the past 25 years?	What has been the impact of policy change over the past 25 years?
Which policies have been introduced to support childcare and early education initiatives recently?	How has childcare and early education been influenced by recent policy?

Critical thinking has been described by Diane Halpern (1996) as:

> thinking that is purposeful, reasoned, and goal directed – the kind of thinking involved in solving problems, formulating inferences, calculating likelihoods, and making decisions when the thinker is using skills that are thoughtful and effective.
>
> (Halpern, 1996)

The emphasis is on thinking that alludes to the student pausing and considering not only the topic or subject in hand but also the questions generated from taking an opportunity to ask those critical rather than factual questions.

To think critically signifies the ability to use a higher order skill that enables professionals to act in a rational and reasonable manner, using empathy and understanding of others in a specific context, such as an early years setting. The rights and needs of others are always the priority, rather than blindly following established procedures.

A critical thinker:

- raises vital questions and problems, formulating them clearly and precisely; gather and assess relevant information, using abstract ideas to interpret it effectively;

- reaches well-reasoned conclusions and solutions, testing them against relevant criteria and standards;

- thinks open-mindedly within alternative systems of thought, recognizing and assessing, as need be, their assumptions, implications, and practical consequences;

- communicates effectively with others in figuring out solutions to complex problems.

(Paul and Elder, 2008)

Alec Fisher (2001) examines the description given by John Dewey of what he termed 'reflective thinking as active, persistent and careful consideration of a belief or supposed form of knowledge in the light of the grounds which support it and further conclusions to which it tends'. Rather than rushing to discover what you believe to be *the answer*, consider disentangling the question and the *right answer* before stating your conclusion. Could there be more to find by turning your factual question into a critical question?

Below are examples of a student discussing her recent visit to another early years setting. The first question is what King (1995) describes as a factual question, and you can see we have highlighted exactly where the facts are in the answer. The second question is a critical question (King, 1995), and again we have highlighted in the answer where the critical elements are.

Question (factual)

What did you see in the new setting that is different from your setting?

> The equipment that was out didn't seem a lot [FCT], in my setting we have everything out [FCT] so the children can access it all, you know like continuous provision. In the other setting they had bare shelves [FCT] and they told me that new equipment was only brought out when the children had mastered those already out [FCT]. They didn't seem to be bothered about the EYFS either, like nothing in the planning was linked to the EYFS [FCT].

(Early childhood studies student, 2013)

Question (critical)

Consider the two different approaches, in your setting and the one that you visited. What impact do you think they have on the children's learning and development?

> I suppose I can see that when we put so much toys and materials out, that there are always children who get things out but don't have a clue how to use it. I guess it would be better if there was less and that the things they did get out were right for the developmental level of each child [CRIT]. I suppose is how we interpret continuous provision [CRIT]. I think as well that the other setting was using the

EYFS to measure the development and learning of each child [CRIT], but they knew the framework and the children well enough not to have to write it all down all the time [CRIT]. They spend most of their time with the children whereas we spend a lot of time sitting writing.

(Early childhood studies student, 2013)

Another example of how you can become a critical thinker might be in asking yourself critical questions as you read and research a topic.

Thought provoking or critical questions require students to go beyond the facts to think about the in ways that are different from what is presented explicitly in class or in the text.

(King, 1995, p 14)

Stella Cottrell (2005) suggests that we must know what we think about a subject and then be able to justify why we think in a certain way: '*having reasons for what we believe...critically evaluating our own beliefs...[and be] able to present to others the reasons for our beliefs and actions*' (Cottrell, 2005, p 3).

Five questions towards critical thinking

1.   Do I understand what I am reading?

2.   Can I explain what I have read (factually)? For example, what is this author telling me about this subject?

3.   What do I think? For example, what is my standpoint, what do I believe is right?

4.   Why do I think that way (critically)? For example, I think that way because I have seen this concept work in practice.

5.   Can I justify to another person my way of thinking?

All that we ask is that you take the time to stop, and consider what you are reading:

What a sad comment on modern educational systems that most learners neither value nor practise active, critical reflection. They are too busy studying to stop and think.

(Hammond and Collins, 1991, p 163)

We encourage you to take time to ask yourself, your peers and your tutors inquisitive and exploratory questions about the topic explored herein, and to stop for a while to move on from the surface level factual questioning for which you will no doubt only find factual answers, and to ponder the wider concepts, the implications to practice and to ask the searching questions to which you may not find such a concrete answer.

For as Van Gelder so eloquently suggests, learning about it is not as useful as doing it:

For students to improve, they must engage in critical thinking itself. It is not enough to learn about critical thinking. These strategies are about as effective as working on your tennis game by watching Wimbledon. Unless the students are actively doing the thinking themselves, they will never improve.

(Van Gelder, 2005, p 43)

References

Cottrell, S (2005) *Critical Thinking Skills*. Basingstoke: Palgrave Macmillan.

Fisher, A (2001) *Critical Thinking: An Introduction*. Cambridge: Cambridge University Press.

Halpern, D F (1996) Thought and Knowledge: An Introduction to Critical Thinking. Mahwah, NJ: Lawrence Erlbaum.

Hammond, M and Collins, R (1991) *Self-Directed Learning: Critical Practice*. London: Kogan Page.

King, A (1995) Designing the Instructional Process to Enhance Critical Thinking across the Curriculum. *Teaching of Psychology*. 22 (1): pp 13–17.

Paul, R and Elder, L (2001) The Miniature Guide to Critical Thinking: Concepts & Tools. Tomales, CA: Foundation Critical Thinking.

Scriven, M and Paul, R (1987) A statement presented at the 8th Annual International Conference on Critical Thinking and Education Reform, Summer 1987.

Van Gelder, T (2005) Teaching Critical Thinking: Some Lessons from Cognitive Science. *College Teaching*. 53 (1): pp 41–48.

1 An introduction to global perspectives of childhood

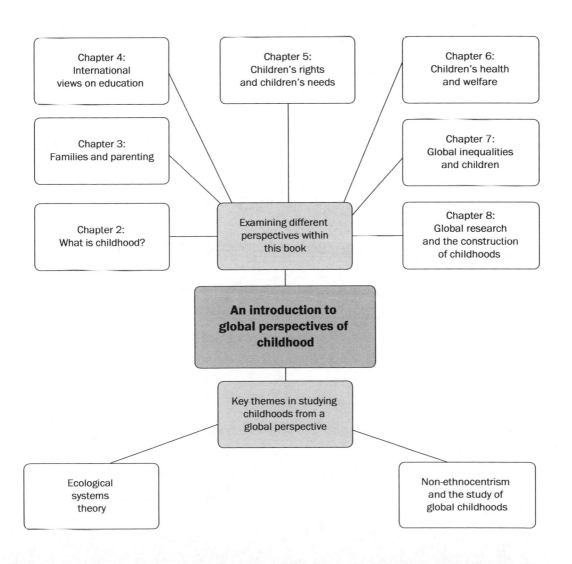

In order to handle the world with maximum competence it is necessary to consider the structure of things. It is necessary to become skilled in manipulating systems and in abstracting forms and patterns. This is a truth which, as a species, we have slowly come to know. If we were ever to renounce the activity, there would be a hefty price to pay.

(Donaldson, 1978, p 82)

Introduction

This chapter examines the key themes that are explored within this book. It identifies the way the study of global childhoods has become an integral part of higher educational studies into childhoods as well as an important aspect of professional practice for those working with children and families. This chapter is divided into two parts:

1. key themes in studying childhoods from a global perspective;

2. examining different perspectives within this book.

The first logical question to consider here is: why study childhoods from a global perspective? A helpful start in answering such a question is to consider how studying childhoods from a global perspective informs your understanding and practice with children and families.

In the quote at the start of this chapter, Margaret Donaldson asserts that maximum competence within this world comes from understanding structures and that only by considering these structures does it become possible to manipulate and abstract form and patterns. This book explores social structures such as families, education, health, welfare and rights. It examines how the patterns of relationships between individuals, institutions and systems influence children's experiences of childhoods. For Donaldson, understanding the foundation structures of things supported the building of higher or intellectual thinking. Contemporary childhoods are not seen as a universal, singular experience but rather as multiple and diverse. Therefore the study of contemporary childhoods considers how the varied experiences of these social structures enable us to explore the ways childhoods are created and lived.

Critical questions

If this study of children and childhoods is to develop our practice, a series of questions arise. Consider your response to these.

» *What structures should we consider in order to achieve a maximum competence in our practice with children and their families?*

» *What factors do you think influence these structures and therefore children's ability to manipulate them?*

» *What skills do children need in order to understand these structures?*

» *What skills will you need in order to understand these structures and abstract forms?*

The complex web of social structures underpinning the world of adults and children is shaped by factors such as gender, race, class, history, economics and politics. The way these influence the interactions between structures, institutions and individuals has long been the subject of debate and argument. Prominent theories emerge, such as a Marxist influence on economic and political structural influences, or Bourdieu's influence on how these factors become embedded in the behaviours of individuals within these structures. In recent times, Margaret Archer's examination of the relationships between social structures and individuals (see Further Reading) has brought the relationship individuals have within these structures to the foreground. The relationships between individuals and the social structures they encounter form the basis of the social systems individuals occupy.

Studying childhoods employing ecological systems theory allows us to examine these social systems through the global networks found in contemporary society. Constraining the examination of these social structures and systems only to that which is familiar and known not only limits understanding of the complexity of the issues surrounding children and childhoods, it also reduces our ability to question these systems in depth. It also risks ignoring those whose experiences of these structures and systems are different (see Chapter 7). In answer to the question: why study childhoods from a global perspective? A suitable answer is: so that you might better understand what shapes childhoods and how you respond to that understanding in order to support individual children within your practice.

Key themes in studying childhoods from a global perspective

If studying childhoods from a global perspective enables us to better analyse the structures and systems that shape those childhoods, then the challenge lies in how best to engage in such a study. Two features fundamental to the study of global childhoods are to recognise the relationships between the social systems and structures and to reflect upon our own response to this. With regard to recognising the relationships between systems and structures, this book will employ the ecological systems theory. With regard to reflecting upon our own response to what analysing these relationships reveals, this book engages the principles of a non-ethnocentric approach to the study of global childhoods.

Ecological systems theory

Ecological systems theory supports analysis of how social structures and social systems interact to influence children's experiences of childhoods. Devised by developmental psychologist Urie Bronfenbrenner, the ecological systems theory (Bronfenbrenner, 1979) identifies five ecological systems that influence an individual child's development. While a child might interact directly with some of these systems, others have their influence without the child ever having direct contact with them. The child's health and gender will be essential aspects that determine how these systems are experienced. The systems are divided into the following.

- *Micro system:* the system the child will have closest direct contact with and includes her/his relationship with institutions such as the family, school, places of worship and local community. The relationships children experience within families and settings are some of the earliest and most influential (see Chapter 7).

- *Meso system:* the system in which micro level institutions interact with each other and are managed within the society. So the relationships between health and education settings and families can influence the experiences of children. In this sense, the relationship professionals have with families can be fundamental to childhood experiences.

- *Exo system:* this is the first system the child will not directly experience, yet it influences his/her childhood. Within this system, structures exist which impact upon the institutions of the micro system. This means that decisions such as local access to health care, employment opportunities and funding of education institutions will affect the child without having any direct contact.

- *Macro system:* this system considers how broader social, cultural, economic and political structures impact upon the child. The cultural and social values of this system influence the other systems. The experiences of children within a nation might differ significantly depending upon economic status, race, culture or religion. Therefore, decisions by national and international institutions of governance and economics, while far removed from the micro level experience, continue to be felt by the child.

- *Chrono system:* the final system relates to the historical influences on children. These might be seen in the short term and relate to the time span of the child's or family's life. However, it also refers to the influence of longer-term historical influences (see Chapter 7 for a discussion of postcolonisation theory).

By using these systems to analyse childhoods from a global perspective, it is possible to explore the interactions between the systems and to compare the differences and similarities within and between nations. However, the ecological systems theory is not without its challenges.

The systems arguably position the child as passive within this process as they predominantly emphasise their impact upon the child. The interactions between these systems do recognise a two-way component, yet this tends to be limited to a reaction to the imposition of decisions and actions made by higher systems. Consequently, the decisions made by a government on educational spending define the reactions those inhabiting the micro system might have to those occupying the macro systems. The child, the family, the teacher are essentially positioned more as individuals who react to what occurs rather than active agents generating their own experiences (this is in some measure addressed within the exo system but it is also bound to remain within that system). Although difficult, there are times when children, as active agents, break through and disrupt these systems, generating and promoting their own ideas. From the examples of Malala Yousafzai, to the agency of Brazilian street working children and the children of sex workers in India (see Chapter 7), and the engagement of 16-year-olds in political debates in the recent Scottish referendum, children as active agents in the micro, meso and macro systems need to be recognised.

Another challenge is the significance placed on the universal elements of the systems. While children might share experiences within and across the systems, to what degree these generate a universal experience is worth exploring. If children are to be seen less as passive recipients and more as active agents then the individual experiences of children must be acknowledged. Social structures of race, class or gender might share similarities in experiences; however, these will be nuanced by the multiple experiences children have. For example, in Chapter 3, US children share with researchers their experiences of growing up in same-sex parented families. They express a desire that social stereotypes of their families or pressure to become *poster children* for same-sex parents does not restrict their abilities to reflect honestly upon their experiences. Clearly, the use of ecological systems theory has value in supporting analysis of global childhoods, yet it is not without its limitations.

Critical questions

»   *Use Bronfenbrenner's ecological systems theory to analyse how the different systems might have influenced your childhood?*

»   *Compare that with an analysis of how these systems might influence a child in your care?*

»   *What, in your opinion, are the advantages and limitations of using the theory in this way?*

»   *As a result of this, how can you utilise this theory in your analysis of global childhoods?*

Non-ethnocentrism and the study of global childhoods

In order to analyse the meaning and implications of non-ethnocentrism, it is necessary to examine what the term ethnocentrism means. Ethnocentrism describes a judgement made of other cultures from one's own perspective. Whether consciously or unconsciously those from the cultural in-group are judged as inherently superior; while those from outside the in-group are judged as deficient and lacking in comparison. LeVine and Campbell (1972) are generally credited with providing a comprehensive system of defining the role and results of ethnocentrism in inter-ethnic relations between cultural groups. However, the term predates this and has been used within anthropological studies since the turn of the twentieth century. The characteristic of judging and finding other cultural groups to be lacking against a standard, which has been defined within one's own cultural group, has been recognised as a universal tendency. However, it has perhaps had its greatest impact in Western and European approaches to non-Western cultures, seen most devastatingly in Western colonialism (see Chapter 7 for an analysis of colonialism and postcolonisation theory). The way in which children learn about culture through a process of inclusion within the group is a defining requisite of all societies. It encompasses not only all aspects of life but, as Kottak (1994) proposes, is so interconnected that if one cultural element within the group changes it will resonate upon the others. The principle behind ethnocentrism lies in creating a single, fixed and unifying in-group identity through exclusion and hostility to other cultural groups.

However, this generalising of ethnocentrism does not reflect the full variations it takes; a greater degree of subtlety in recognising the various forms is necessary in order to support self-reflection. The premise that in-group preference exists through devaluing the out-group cultures, as LeVine and Campbell (1972) suggest, reflects a classic ethnocentrism. Raden (2003) suggests a more subtle range of ethnocentrism is evident through in-group bias which rates one's own culture as higher than others but which does not equate favourable in-group bias with negative out-group judgements. So both in-group and out-group judgements might be negative but the in-group is judged less negatively than the out-group.

There are two reasons for examining the premise of ethnocentrism: first in respect to the way we approach the study of childhoods from a cross-cultural perspective and second, and most significantly, the implications for practice with children and families. When analysing research from a global perspective, taking an ethnocentric stance means the value of what can be learnt from studying different cultural experiences of childhoods will be lost, overshadowed by a prejudgement that finds the actions of families and institutions lacking. Within practice, ethnocentrism results not only in devaluing the heritage of children and families from different cultural groups but also in silencing voices from groups on the grounds that they do not reflect the cultural values within an institution. This not only risks failing to listen and learn from other cultural groups, but it also risks the marginalisation of groups who feel judged as *lacking* within the institution.

If this is to be avoided then an alternative approach needs to be considered. Cultural relativism suggests an answer lies in being able to understand and respect another cultural group's values and ideas. Introduced by anthropologist Franz Boas, cultural relativism offers a means to recognise that there is no single developmental route for all cultural groups. Boas argued that if individuals view the world from their own cultural perspective, understanding comes from recognising and learning from cultural difference rather than through measuring other cultures against one's own. However, this is not without challenges and limitations any less troubling than that of ethnocentrism. As Sanders (2009) discusses, cultural relativism's risks lie in the extremes. If cultural relativism is to be carried to its extreme conclusions then much harm is risked. If cultural groups are to be measured only against their own values and not that of others, it becomes impossible to achieve a foundation of values which would challenge the belief in child witches, slavery, female genital mutilation or any other practices which might be argued as cultural norms within groups. These extremes are frequently cited for their obvious impact as extremes; however, the boundaries between acceptable and unacceptable cultural norms present challenges.

If you are to critically analyse global research into children's experiences, the challenge lies in considering what values are to be used in order to analyse the actions of cultural groups in the research studies. Within your practice the ability to measure where the boundaries between acceptable and unacceptable cultural practices lie sets a challenge between balancing ethnocentrism against cultural relativism.

Taking a non-ethnocentric approach, while in no way providing an *easy answer* to the challenges of ethnocentrism and extreme cultural relativism, does suggest the need to tread a path between these conflicting ideas. These challenges are presented not only to students engaging in cross-cultural studies and to practitioners working with children and families in contemporary culturally and socially diverse communities, they are also challenges that large international organisations such as the United Nations must face. In creating and implementing a set of universal rights for children across the world, the United Nations Convention on the Rights of the Child (UNCRC) presents a vehicle by which a non-ethnocentric approach might be guided (see Chapter 5 for an examination of the UNCRC). While this is not a definitive answer it does provide a starting point to support self-reflection upon your own cultural values and ideas. Taking a non-ethnocentric approach does not mean denying one's own cultural identity and values, nor does it mean taking a purely objective approach to the study of global childhoods (if such objectivity were to be considered possible), rather it tasks one to examine one's own cultural values and to approach the analysis of cross-cultural studies with an awareness of what can be learnt to support one's own knowledge and practice.

However, seeking to understand different cultural groups comes with two important caveats. The first is presented through postcolonisation theory which offers a warning that seeking to compare different cultural groups is a complex process that requires an understanding of historical contexts. The second challenges the process of seeking to understand different cultural groups against one's own understanding. However well-intentioned, this invariably risks undermining that which is unique and essentially unknowable of that group. This *Othering* of cultural groups as well as a discussion of postcolonisation theory is explored further in Chapter 7. (See MacNaughton in Further Reading to examine these issues and their relevance to the study of childhoods and practice with children).

Critical questions

» *Use the results following the analysis of your childhood influences using Bronfenbrenner's ecological systems theory to analyse the cultural values you hold.*

» *How might these impact upon your ability to take a non-ethnocentric approach to the study of global childhoods?*

» *Reflect upon how this shapes your practice with children and families.*

» *What, in your opinion, are the advantages and limitations of engaging a non-ethnocentric approach to your study of global childhoods and your practice?*

The case study below offers the opportunity to apply these theories to an analysis of the experiences of childcare time that lone and partnered mothers have across four nations.

CASE STUDY

Craig, L and Mullan, K (2012) Lone and Partnered Mothers' Childcare Time within Context in Four Countries. European Sociological Review. 28 (4): pp 512–526.

Within this study the researchers compared and contrasted lone and partnered mothers' childcare time in four countries which hold social norms and policies towards mothers and childcare, and family and work. The countries were Australia, the United States, France and Denmark.

The researchers explored social norms of what constituted *good mothering* and national policies on practical support such as affordable childcare. For lone mothers this was particularly relevant as they were more likely to have fewer resources, including time, than partnered mothers. The researchers found that partnered mothers in the two Anglo countries spent substantially more time with their children than the two European nations. This was seen as reflecting cultural norms regarding mothering roles. However, the comparison with lone mothers was starker. All countries showed that lone mothers spent less time in childcare activities than partnered mothers. The widest gap between partnered and lone mothers' childcare time was seen in the United States. The researchers linked this with the reduced welfare provision available to lone mothers in the United States compared to other nations. The next widest gap was in France, followed by Australia, with Denmark having the least difference in childcare time between partnered and lone mothers. Lone mothers in the United States were spending childcare time that was closest in comparison to the lone mothers in France and Denmark. In Denmark, lone mothers' employment was higher than in the United States; however, their access to welfare support and supplemented childcare was also higher than in the United States. In France a social norm towards a collectivist approach to childcare led to higher state support for supplemented childcare for both partnered and lone mothers who were more likely to be in employment.

The study demonstrates how cultural norms regarding the role of mothers and the support governments offer in the form of supplemented childcare or welfare provision differ across four nations.

Critical questions

Consider the following questions in relation to the case study.

»   *Using Bronfenbrenner's ecological systems theory, how are macro and meso level decisions impacting the micro level experiences of mothers and children?*

»   *How are different cultural norms shaping ideas of motherhood within these nations?*

»   *What, in your opinion, might be the consequences of how government policies influence the ways lone and partnered mothers experience cultural norms of motherhood?*

»   *How do cultural norms of motherhood and government policies influence the experiences of children and families in your practice?*

Examining different perspectives within this book

Let us now examine the approach this book takes to global perspectives of childhood. A global perspective of childhood enables historical, social and cultural understanding of children to be analysed in a greater depth and to critique the notion of a universal child and childhood.

In addition, looking within and beyond a Western perspective reveals the impact that gender, class and race have had, and continue to have, on shaping childhood experiences.

While each chapter in the book can be used as a stand-alone discussion of an aspect of childhood, it also builds to create an overall view of aspects important to the study of childhoods from a global perspective.

Chapter 2: What is childhood?

Chapter 2 poses this question which has no clear and simple answer as it is premised on numerous experiences, values and viewpoints. However, taking different viewpoints around this question supports a basis for interesting dialogues.

- Taking a historical perspective means asking how childhoods have been constructed and examined throughout history.

- From the premise that the concept of childhood is one that has not always been visible in societies, to the way social values have shaped what constitutes a good childhood, the examination of childhood has tended to centre upon Western childhoods. Taking a non-Western historical view reveals how colonialism impacted upon childhoods to create ideas of non-Western childhoods that impact upon children today.

- Taking a contemporary approach to answering this question reveals how childhood has become a social construct, influenced by factors of race, class and gender. These factors shape children's experiences of childhoods through the creation of identity. Identity is arguably a fluid and complex concept that comprises in-group identity as examined not only in the discussion on non-ethnocentrism but also from positioning of that group identity in relation to wider society as examined through social systems theory. Yet it is also subject to individual identity which is adaptable and changes to fit within the different social and cultural spaces children inhabit and experience. Children's agency suggests that children are not passively shaped by their experiences but rather react and shape not only their own identity but to a greater or lesser degree that of those around them.

The view adults have of childhood is both shaped by their own adult values and their childhood experiences. This is significant both in respect to how they then view children and childhoods today and how these views impact upon contemporary childhood experiences.

Chapter 3: Families and parenting

A global view of families and child-rearing is examined in Chapter 3. Definitions of families have been given by the United Nations (United Nations Statistics Division, 2013); yet the roles families play in childhoods are not so easily categorised. The family, as a unit, is often the first and dominant space in which children experience their childhoods. This space has been, and remains, the subject of cultural, political and historical debate. Aspects such as gendered and transgendered roles in society, economic instability and population migration have resulted in the diverse constructions of families becoming a global phenomenon. The

UN's desire to define and categorise these changes in family structure serves to further reinforce their importance within societies.

One such change to family structure that has become a feature within contemporary Western societies is same-sex parented families. Research by Welsh (2011) with children from same-sex parented families in the United States reflects how their childhood experiences of negotiating prejudice and identity challenge any simplistic comparisons between their families and heterosexual families.

Another important aspect in any discussion of families will be the roles of parents in shaping childhoods. John Bowlby's attachment theory has become an integral part of this discussion. Taking a global view of attachment theory reveals the debate about how the theory can be *translated* into culturally diverse situations. This leads to a discussion about how much cultural variations influence not only this theory but also the way parents transmit values and cultural norms. Ideas of what constitutes *good* parenting benefit from cross-cultural analysis in order to recognise how changing social and cultural norms not only influence the form families take but also the roles adults and children play within the family. This is most starkly illustrated in a study by Francis-Chizororo (2010) into child-headed households in Zimbabwe (an occurrence which is likely to rise in communities devastated by the recent ebola outbreak in West Africa).

Chapter 4: International views on education

Education has become one of the most powerful tools a nation has to develop children's individual intellectual skills, shape them into national citizens and prepare them to become workers in a global economy. To this end, education has, arguably, become a global commodity subject to international pressures and restraints. From an international position as one of the rights of the child, it is now a powerful defining force in contemporary global childhoods.

International organisations such as the United Nations Educational, Scientific and Cultural Organization (UNESCO) and the Organisation for Economic Cooperation and Development (OECD) have developed systems which now shape national education policies. Early childhood education has become one of the areas of most rapid development within education as it becomes a space where nations not only seek to gain advantage by preparing young children for later education, but it is also seen increasingly as a means to address broader social issues through early intervention.

These changes have led to a convergence of education systems. Standardised testing, for example, has developed as a means to promote accountability in teaching and learning, and has become an important aspect of these convergent global education systems. The increasing importance placed on the outcomes of these tests has led to easily measured, factual knowledge becoming the driving force dominating less measurable skills such as attitudes to learning. To what degree standardised testing improves the education of all children, particularly the least advantaged, and whether it improves the quality of the curriculum or teaching, are also considered.

Chapter 5: Children's rights and children's needs

That children have rights as well as needs has become part of the lexicon of contemporary childhoods. It is a general view that children's rights comprise three broad strands – provision, protection and participation. Examining the historical journey demonstrates how the modern children's rights agenda emerged from nineteenth-century European welfare reform (Fuchs, 2008) to the United Nations Convention on the Rights of the Child (UNCRC) (UN, 1989). The African Charter on the Rights and Welfare of the Child (ACRWC) builds upon the UNCRC as the only region-specific rights charter to address the specific rights and needs of children on the African continent and has created specific rights from risks to girls of female genital mutilation (FGM) and early marriage, to defining a child within African cultural concepts of community, duties and responsibilities.

The needs of children have resulted in a general acceptance and legitimacy of actions conducted by governments and international organisations in the name of children's needs, adding an element of power to policies and policy-makers aimed at addressing these needs. This creates what Bûhler-Niederberger (2003, p 95) terms the naturalisation of the *needy child* who, unlike the *useful child*, does not contribute to family income but is rendered economically *useless*, as fits a Western view of childhood. Yet there is a complication that, from a Western rights perspective, the *useful child* risks exploitation; however, the ACRWC reflects how the *needy child* model of childhood also sits at odds with a view that children should have responsibilities to their family and community.

Chapter 6: Children's health and welfare

Children's health and welfare have become such ubiquitous terms that they are seldom examined and questioned. While the World Health Organization's (WHO) definition of health as: '*a state of complete physical, mental and social well-being and not merely the absence of disease or infirmity*' (WHO, 1946, p 100) presents a micro level view of health, public health refers more to macro level measures promoting health, preventing disease and prolonging life in populations as a whole and does not focus on individual people or diseases (WHO, 2013). Welfare in micro level terms is generally seen as personal well-being, whereas in meso and macro level terms it frequently refers to economic and financial support provided by a state or international organisation. Welfare exists from both an economic and sociological viewpoint.

Key international organisations such as the United Nations Children's Fund (UNICEF), the World Bank and the International Monetary Fund (IMF) have, in the past two decades, managed their role in children's health and welfare through the United Nations Millennium Development Goals (MDGs). The MDGs have shaped development and aid distribution aimed at achieving set targets by 2015. In 2014 a set of 17 Sustainable Development Goals (SDGs) aim to continue the work of the MDGs post-2015. These goals reflect the changing influences on children's health and welfare, including the fact that the majority of the world's poor now live in middle income nations. It is worth noting that MDG 6 (combat HIV/AIDS, malaria and other diseases) reflected the concern for effective management of infectious diseases such as the HIV/AIDS epidemic; however, the post-2015 development agenda contains no specific provision regarding HIV/AIDS or other communicable diseases, and it is instead subsumed within SDG 3 (ensure healthy lives and promote well-being for all at all ages). As the ebola epidemic raises concerns internationally, the removal of a specific disease management goal might appear short-sighted. Indeed, as child mortality rates fall, the ensuing rise in the cost of health provision and education means, as Atisophon et al (2011, p 48) point out, that *'financing health and education expenditures is not identical to ensuring health and education outcomes'*.

Chapter 7: Global inequalities and children

An increasingly important area of global childhood studies is the way inequalities between and within nations impact upon children in terms of both opportunities and outcomes (OECD, 2008). The economic difficulties in global markets in 2008 illustrate how global economic uncertainty and rising fuel and food prices impact most heavily upon those already living on the global economic margins. Inequalities of wealth mean low income nations are impacted by economic crises which decrease trade and reduce expenditure by wealthier nations on aid budgets. Applying an ecological perspective illustrates how macro level economic problems transfer to the micro level where children in families who lack resources to buffer themselves from economic hardship become particularly vulnerable.

One result of economic inequality is a rise in urbanisation. This does not necessarily mean migration into large, well-established cities; smaller cities and large towns also experience influx from rural areas and may be less able to cope. However, a rise in urban populations does offer new possibilities for development through centralising of resources and services, and can bring advantages over services scattered across rural communities. In addition, urbanisation offers opportunities for social mobility and empowerment, particularly for women (Martine, 2007).

Gender inequality presents the greatest inequality that children face and is evident across all nations, both rich and poor. Women from poor communities bear the greatest burden as rising unemployment means women are most likely to be in poorly paid, less secure work that requires them to spend longer time away from their children. This often results in girls leaving education early to care for younger siblings. Yet, while children are frequently distanced from decisions that impact their lives, children do demonstrate agency, often through their engagement in political activism that challenge the dyadic roles of the child as decision-recipient and the adult as decision-maker.

Chapter 8: Global research and the construction of childhoods

Research with and on children generates important questions for those who wish to learn from the findings of these studies. The twentieth and twenty-first centuries have seen international research on children and childhoods expand, with the emergence of communication technology that makes longitudinal, international, macro level studies examining childhoods possible. Research offers opportunities to understand children's multiple and diverse experiences of childhood in increasingly relevant and meaningful ways, both through *big* data, macro level transnational studies, to micro level studies of issues impacting individual children, their families and their communities. Yet international child research with and on children is not without challenges: ethical questions asked include why research is conducted on, with or by children. The power imbalance that exists between adult researcher and child participant is inevitably bound with wider discourses around the ethics of the relationship between wealthy minority world nations and less wealthy majority world nations. The ethical principles to ensure non-maleficence within research studies oblige researchers to ensure the research encounter benefits the children who are directly or indirectly involved. However, engaging in studies frequently results in researchers facing ethical decision-making dilemmas.

Seeing children as active agents within their lives and communities leads to them being seen as more active participants in international and global child research. *Children as researchers* moves beyond a view of children as participants who offer *insider perspectives* into children who design, conduct and disseminate research with the support of adults. Children's active engagement in research offers the opportunity for issues which impact upon their lives to be explored in ways which adults are unable to conceive.

Further reading

Archer, M (2007) *Making Our Way through the World: Human Reflexivity and Social Mobility*. Cambridge: Cambridge University Press. For a thought-provoking analysis of the place and role of reflexivity in contemporary society.

MacNaughton, G (2005) *Doing Foucault in Early Childhood Studies*. London: Routledge. Offers a comprehensive examination of the study of childhoods from a cross-cultural perspective.

References

Atisophon, V, Bueren, J, De Paepe, G, Garroway, C and Stijns, J (2011) Revisiting MDG Cost Estimates From a Domestic Resource Mobilisation Perspective. Working Paper No. 306. Paris: OECD.

Bronfenbrenner, U (1979) *The Ecology of Human Development. Experiments by Nature and Design*. Cambridge MA: Harvard University Press.

Bühler-Niederberger, D (2003) The Needy Child and the Naturalization of Politics: Political Debate in Germany, in Hallett, C and Prout, A (eds) *Hearing the Voices of Children*. Abingdon: Routledge.

Craig, L and Mullan, K (2012) Lone and Partnered Mothers' Childcare Time within Context in Four Countries. *European Sociological Review*. 28 (4): pp 512–526.

Donaldson, M (1978) *Children's Minds*. London: HarperCollins.

Francis-Chizororo, M (2010) Growing Up without Parents: Socialisation and Gender Relations in Orphaned-Child-Headed Households in Rural Zimbabwe. *Journal of Southern African Studies*. 36 (3): pp 711–727.

Fuchs, E (2008) Children's Rights and Global Civil Society. *Comparative Education*. 43 (3): pp 398–412.

Kottak, C (1994) *Cultural Anthropology*. New York: McGraw Hill.

LeVine, R and Campbell, D (1972) *Ethnocentrism: Theories of Conflict, Ethnic Attitudes and Group Behavior*. New York: Wiley.

Martine, G (2007) *State of World Population 2007: Unleashing the Potential of Urban Growth*. London: United Nations Population Fund.

OECD (2008) *Growing Unequal? Income Distribution and Poverty in OECD Countries*. Paris: OECD Publishing.

Raden, D (2003) Ingroup Bias, Classic Ethnocentrism and Non-ethnocentrism Among American Whites. *Political Psychology*. 24 (4): pp 803–808.

Sanders, B (2009) Childhood in Different Cultures, in Maynard, T and Thomas, N (eds) *An Introduction to Early Childhood Studies*. London: Sage.

UN (1989) Declaration of the Rights of the Child. [online] Available at: www.un.org (accessed 24 July 2014).

United Nations Statistics Division (2013) Households and Families. [online] Available at: http://unstats. un.org/unsd/demographic/sconcerns/fam/fammethods.htm#A2 (accessed 10 April 2014).

Welsh, G (2011) Growing Up in a Same-Sex Parented Family: The Adolescent Voice of Experience. *Journal of GLBT Family Studies*. 7 (1–2): pp 49–71.

WHO (1946) *Preamble to the Constitution of the World Health Organization as Adopted by the International Health Conference*. New York: Official Records of the World Health Organization.

WHO (2013) Mental Health: A State of Well-Being. [online] Available at: www.who.int/features/factfiles/ mental_health/en/ (accessed 3 August 2014).

2 What is childhood?

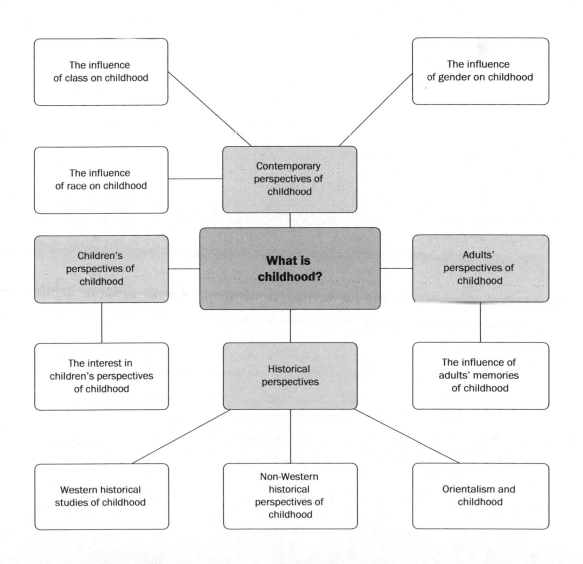

The influence of class on childhood

The influence of gender on childhood

The influence of race on childhood

Contemporary perspectives of childhood

Children's perspectives of childhood

What is childhood?

Adults' perspectives of childhood

The interest in children's perspectives of childhood

Historical perspectives

The influence of adults' memories of childhood

Western historical studies of childhood

Non-Western historical perspectives of childhood

Orientalism and childhood

This vision of a 'century of the child' attracted reformers for most of the first half of the twentieth century. Their overriding aim was to map out a territory called 'childhood', and put in place frontier posts which would prevent too early an escape from what was seen as desirably a garden of delight.

(Cunningham, 2005, p 172)

Introduction

This chapter provides a discussion of the various perspectives that have emerged from asking '*what is childhood?*'. Ultimately it is a question that is impossible to answer, but by exploring the possibilities that arise from this question new insights can emerge.

This chapter is divided into four parts:

1. historical perspectives of childhood;

2. contemporary perspectives of childhood;

3. adults' perspectives of childhood;

4. children's perspectives of childhood.

Much of the way Western societies view childhood is through a lens that sees childhood as a time of vulnerability in need of protection. This chapter studies how this understanding of childhoods has become embedded within societies and the lives of those individuals within them.

Historical perspectives

In the quote at the start of the chapter Cunningham (2005) refers to the twentieth century as the *century of the child*, an idea proposed by Ellen Key in her book *The Century of the Child* published in English in 1909. Cunningham goes on to describe how this led early-twentieth-century reformers to view childhood as an idyll to be protected and shielded (See Nutbrown et al, 2009, for an interesting and alternative study of the pioneers who have shaped our understanding of childhood throughout history).

Critical questions

»   *Research how social and educational reformers such as Rachel and Margaret McMillan, Susan Isaacs and John Dewey have contributed to this view of childhood.*

»   *In what ways have prominent child development theorists such as John Bowlby and Jean Piaget contributed to this view of childhood?*

»   *Compare these views of childhood to that taken in the United Nations Convention on the Rights of the Child (UNCRC) (United Nations, 1989). How are they similar and how do they differ?*

»   *How do these views of childhood stand up to scrutiny in the early twenty-first century?*

Western historical studies of childhood

Any discussion of the historical perspective of childhood is undoubtedly shaped by three influential Western historians: Phillippe Ariès (1962), Lloyd deMause (1974) and Edward Shorter (1977). Their studies marked a growing interest in how a historical examination of the traditionally less visible social lives of ordinary men, women and children might inform the study of contemporary society. What emerged were the often contested discourses of historical childhoods, leading to a premise that prior to the eighteenth century, concepts of childhood were vague and ill-defined, lacking any clear notion of the point at which a child left childhood and entered the adult world. Usefully these ideas led to debates, particularly by deMause (1974), that studying the historical treatment of children reveals much about the way the contemporary adult world has come to view childhood.

Certainly, studying the history of the emergence of an idea of childhood demonstrates the influence that social and cultural values had and continue to have on the premise of what childhood is and should be. As Lowe (2005) describes, European history shows the ways in which notions of childhoods have been framed from two opposing views of children. The first, heavily influenced by Christian doctrine on original sin, saw the needs of the body as secondary to the needs of the immortal soul. Such a viewpoint positioned children as intrinsically evil and in need of redemption in order to protect their souls. This frequently occurred at the expense of the body and influenced ideas of childhood for centuries. The second historical influence on childhoods also reflects Christian ideology of children; however, rather than intrinsically evil, children become innocents in need of protection from the corrupting influence of the adult world. Indeed this view can be seen embedded in the quote that started this chapter. These ideas continue to trouble contemporary views of childhood, particularly at times when the actions of children cause society to question its view of childhoods, for example the criminalisation of children.

At this point it is important to introduce a caveat. Much of what is written about childhood histories take a Western perspective. Arguably, answering the question at the start of this chapter 'what is childhood?' is likely to be framed by European ideas. The childhoods Aries, deMause and Shorter speak of are Western childhoods.

Non-Western historical perspectives of childhood

The histories of childhood that emerge from Aries and his contemporaries are based on European studies seen through a Western lens, the childhoods Cunningham (2005) refers to at the start of this chapter. However, non-Western nations also have histories of childhoods. Globally the histories of these childhoods are less easily heard. Let us take as an example a historical perspective of childhoods in India.

Study of the histories of childhoods in India draws on aspects of postcolonisation theories (see Chapter 7 for an analysis of postcolonisation theories) and Orientalism to analyse the way these histories impact upon modern Indian childhoods. Said's (1978) definitive work on Orientalism analysed how the Western understanding of diverse Eastern nations and cultures has resulted in the creation of an often homogenised grouping of people that speaks more of the prejudices of the West than of any attempt at a meaningful understanding of the peoples of those nations. However, Said's views have been sharply criticised, not least for perpetuating a Western critique of Eastern nations rather than focussing on the subjects of Orientalism and their own representation of themselves and their histories. Indeed Orientalism continues to inform the debate of how Western and non-Western nations are defined, particularly in the twenty-first century (Kumar, 2012).

Orientalism and childhood

Balagoplan (2002), in a study of a vocational education programme in India, examines how precolonial childhoods, while influenced by systems of caste, were not built on notions of child labour beyond domestic work. It was only with the colonisation of India by the British that formal paid child labour emerged. While nineteenth-century reformers in Britain saw legislation abolish child labour, the same was not forthcoming in Indian childhoods. Balagoplan (2002) argues that these childhoods were further influenced by an education system constructed by the British during imperial rule to privilege an elite few in Indian society and which created further divisions within Indian childhoods. The development of a standardised education system, rather than creating egalitarian opportunities, promoted the childhoods of the elite while marginalising the childhoods of the poor. Echoing deMause's premise that by studying how the historical treatment of children shaped adult societies and informs the way we understand childhood, Balagoplan (2002) concludes that studying the histories of Indian childhoods reveals much about contemporary childhoods in India from a non-Westernised viewpoint.

Critical questions

This chapter begins with a question – 'what is childhood?'. Having read about the historical perspectives of childhood, reflect upon your initial thoughts when presented with this question.

» *How might historical notions of childhood influence your views on contemporary childhood issues such as play, the media and technology?*

» *Why do you think there is a tendency to focus on Western ideas when seeking answers to these issues?*

» *What can the study of non-Western histories teach us about childhood?*

» *How might your answers challenge the way you now approach the study of childhoods?*

The study of children's historical experiences suggests that the century of the child emerged from prior centuries of childhoods framed by Western societies; the *garden of delight* that Cunningham (2005, p 172) described was clearly not open to all. This leads to the discussion of how childhood as a social construct is influenced by the same factors that influence wider society. This is a discourse that dominates contemporary discussions about childhood.

Contemporary perspectives of childhood

If childhood is to be considered as a social construct, which contemporary perspectives of childhood invariably do, then this idea of a social construction requires further examination. The social construction of childhood refers to the meaning given to childhood by the expectations society places on it. So, for example, the previous section discussed how Western societies' view of what childhood is and what it should look like has shaped the construction of childhood through the last two centuries and into contemporary rhetoric. This is significant because the combined influence of globalisation and technology means there is a far wider reach for such ideas.

If Western perspectives dominate contemporary social constructions of childhood, they do not do so unchallenged. The rise in prominence of studying childhood from an international, cross-cultural perspective has become part of the lexicon of contemporary studies of childhood. As Sanders (2009, p 10) so neatly phrases it, the practitioner working with children in contemporary society 'needs not only to learn "what works?", but "what works for this particular child, from this particular socioeconomic and cultural background"'. Being open to social influences beyond Western ones not only expands the practical skills of practitioners but also supports a non-ethnocentric approach to the study of childhood. In doing so, the practitioner can recognise that there is something to be learnt from different approaches to childhoods and the social ideas that influence them. First, however, let us examine identity as a fundamental way in which these factors influence childhood experiences.

Much of the discussion of how race, class and gender impact on the construction of childhoods considers how they influence children's personal identity. All children have a gender, racial and class identity; the relevance of studying these factors is to examine how these macro level factors impact on the micro level and a child's identity and childhood experiences. The study of identity can be seen as composed of *hard* and *soft* elements (Brubaker, 2004). *Hard* elements suggest a fundamental core identity that remains fixed over time. Alternatively, the *soft* elements suggest an understanding of identity that is fluid, changing and adapting from experience and over time. These two elements reflect a changing approach to the study of identity. Historically, Brubaker (2004) proposes that identity, particularly identity linked to race, class and gender, was seen in terms of how a group was positioned within wider society. Racial identity for a minority group, for example, is shaped predominantly by the fact that they are positioned outside the dominant social identity. Contemporary studies of identity are more likely to focus on the multiplicity of identity (Butler-Sweet, 2011) that reflects the influence of multiple sources of identity. Identity, it is argued, cannot be seen as fixed but rather it is adaptive to the circumstances a person exists within.

While the influences of race, class and gender impact holistically on the social construction of childhood, it is worth considering the particular macro level influence each of these can have. The first factor to be considered is race.

The influence of race on childhood

Historically, race has been construed as a means of categorising groups of people based on observable and unobservable biological characteristics such as skin colour, physical features and genes. Ethnicity has become the means by which cultural characteristics such as language and religion are apportioned to groups of people with shared ancestors. Both race and ethnicity have social meaning. The categorising of a person based on race and ethnicity has an impact with real effects on those making the judgement as well as those being judged.

State bureaucracy typically uses race and ethnicity to classify individuals and communities in order to measure and monitor society. Within Western societies the data provided are frequently used to evidence, for example, the racial identities of populations in local communities, schools, prisons and professions. Therefore, the racial and ethnic characteristics socially ascribed to groups of people both from outside and within that community will influence the childhood experiences of children. Stone and Dolbin-MacNab (2013) posit that for parents of children from biracial or multiracial families completing ethnic identity forms may present choices that do not accurately reflect their family's racial identity and necessitate making a choice that may elevate one parent's racial identity while diminishing the others. This demonstrates the role of social cognition in influencing how children's formation of racial and ethnic identity develops, in part, through interactions with other social and racial groups.

Social cognition suggests that an individual's perception, judgements and behaviour towards others is influenced by the beliefs that form part of their personal identity. For children, social cognition of race comes from internal identity and external social clues. The study below explores this further; researchers examined how African American children use social experience and racial attitudes to form expectations of whether they might experience discrimination.

CASE STUDY

Rowley, J, Burchinal, M, Roberts, J and Zeisel, S (2008) Racial Identity, Social Context, and Race-Related Social Cognition in African Americans during Middle Childhood. Developmental Psychology. *44 (6): pp 1537–1546.*

Seventy-three African American children participated in a study conducted following their completion of third grade (when they were aged between eight and nine years of age) and fifth grade (when they were aged between ten and eleven years of age). The researchers used a racial story task. Four vignettes read to the children involved short stories of cross-racial situations. All the characters in the stories, teachers, peers and school administrators, were European American except the main character who was African American and the same age and gender as the child listening to the story. An example included asking the child to decide who the teacher would choose if an African American child and a European American child both raised their hand to answer a question, and participants were asked to explain why they made that decision.

On average the children in third grade used race discrimination as the explanation when deciding on negative social outcomes from the vignettes. By the fifth grade, however, despite research suggesting that perceptions of discrimination are more prevalent at this age, the children in the study showed a small but significant decrease in the use of racial discrimination to explain negative social outcomes from the vignettes. The researchers concluded that between the ages of eight and nine the children demonstrated an understanding of race discrimination that meant African Americans like themselves might experience negative social outcomes. However, by the time the children were aged between ten and eleven this had become more subtle and the children's understanding of the situations showed more sophistication that reflected the children's understanding of the role and intricacies of friendships with children of the same and different races.

The researchers did not claim that a study of this size could be expanded as representative of all African American school children. The study does suggest, however, that on the micro level those children for whom race was a high central component of their self-identity were more acutely aware of the possibilities that they might experience racial discrimination. These can be linked to previous studies that suggest that having a strong racial identity, though making children and young people more likely to expect to experience discrimination, also acts as a buffer when experiencing negative social outcomes. In addition, children who thought others held positive views of African Americans were more likely to anticipate positive social interactions.

Critical questions

Reflecting on the study above and the conclusions the researchers drew from their analysis consider the following questions.

»   *What do the ideas being discussed suggest about broader social views and attitudes to race in the United States?*

»   *What conclusions might we draw from the study about how these children were developing their racial identities?*

»   *How does this compare and contrast with your practice and experience?*

While race can be seen as a factor that influences the social construction of contemporary childhoods, it can also be linked with other aspects. Class is frequently linked with race as a factor that shapes children's experiences of childhood. This is the next factor to consider.

The influence of class on childhood

Contemporary discussions on class broadly identify it in terms of economic wealth and social capital. It is these resources, or the lack of them, and their influence on childhoods that form the focus of much that is written and researched about class. Remember that class interacts with the other factors of race and gender in both subtle and obvious ways (for examples and in-depth examination of these see Chapter 7). A deeper evaluation of how race and gender influence childhoods needs to recognise the impact class has on these factors. However, when class is seen in purely economic terms, its relationship with childhood can become overwhelmed by discussions on family income, welfare and aid provision. Indeed in Western childhood literature much is written about the impact of socio-economic levels and children's social capital in terms of accessing and flourishing in education and health. So, for example, discussions about boys' engagement with literacy is further analysed in terms of race and class, leading to more focused and structured programmes for encouraging engagement. These are, of course, important areas that necessitate careful examination and often act as drivers of governments' education policies. Particularly at times of economic uncertainty, analysis of class in terms of wealth can lead to strong responses based on class identity often presented through the media and government policies on welfare and pay.

However, the micro level experiences of how class influences childhoods reveal more intimate analysis. The experience of children within the middle class of South Korea is explored below. South Korea has undergone a cultural shift over recent decades. The influence of Western ideas through globalisation and the country's rapid economic expansion means that traditional Korean cultural collectivist values are being shaped by the incoming Western individualist values.

Within societies it is often the upper middle classes that lead changes in cultural values that influence childhoods; they are likely to lead new trends in education and child-rearing practices that will later influence the rest of society. South Korea is experiencing a period of social transformation which means traditional cultural ideals coexist with newly imported Western cultural trends. The two cultures are sharply diverse: traditional Korean culture values collectivist ideals while Western cultural values focus on individualism. This leads to social upheaval as people change and acclimatise to new cultural traditions. Within Korean society it is the upper middle classes who experience this inflowing Western culture first, and who also experience the challenges this brings.

CASE STUDY

Park, J and Young, I (2009) Parental Goals and Parenting Practices of Upper-Middle-Class Korean Mothers with Preschool Children. Journal of Early Childhood Research. *7 (1): pp 58–75.*

Park and Young (2009) report inconsistencies between what upper middle class mothers thought about child-rearing and what they reported they actually did. The mothers had all stated that good social and emotional characteristics were their main parenting objectives, consistent with traditional Korean collectivist cultural values. However, while the mothers described the importance of social and emotional development, their child-rearing practice concentrated mostly on educating their children in preparation for starting primary schooling. The mothers reported spending most of their time with their children in studying and teaching reading, writing, mathematics and English, including hiring personal tutors to help with this. While some mothers were concerned with the impact this might have on their children, they felt the social pressure to continue with these practices in order not to disadvantage their child. This did not mean parents were not helping their children with their social and emotional development, but that the greatest priority these mothers placed was on their children's academic development.

It appears that within this *unsettled period* that South Korea is experiencing, as their society adapts to a mixture of two different cultural ideals, it is the upper middle classes that lead the way.

The research highlights the way class influences childhoods at the micro level. The macro level experience of cultural change within South Korean society might be the driver, but it is within the upper middle class families that this is being interpreted. Therefore the way these Korean mothers translate what individualised Western values mean for their children is being influenced not just by their culture but also their class. These mothers are seeking to prepare their children to be able to compete within the upper classes of a rapidly changing Korean society.

Critical questions

Use these questions to critique the case study above.

» *What does the case study suggest about South Korean childhoods in the future?*

» *What does this research tell you about the role class plays in influencing childhoods?*

» *How does this case study inform your analysis of making comparisons of childrens' educational achievements between nations?*

» *Why might the trend in research on race, class and gender focus on the negative impacts they have on the childhoods children experience?*

The influence of gender on childhood

The influence gender has on childhoods, like class and race, cannot be seen in isolation. Yet the study of gender builds a more nuanced understanding of childhoods and children's identity. As with the discussion of race and class, much of the discussion of gender and its impact upon childhoods has focused on how it reproduces inequalities. As Wells (2009) notes, this risks the premise that gender like race is something that is done to children, positioning children as empty vessels. Children's agency in this regard will be discussed later in this chapter; however, the limitations of viewing children as passive in regard to developing a gendered identity risks seeing gender identity in purely biological terms.

Examining the influence of gender on childhoods requires a greater depth of analysis. If the sex of a child is determined by biology, the gender identity a child develops is influenced by a myriad of social influences. Gender as a social construct permeates societies and cannot be separated into the distinct social spheres children might inhabit. So gender permeates family roles, care, education and labour; it is shaped by the impact of globalisation, technology and media, and it is both influenced by and influences race, class and sexuality. It is within these spheres that children learn and construct their understanding of gender identity. Given this premise, a simple binary of gender identity as male or female seems too restrictive, unlikely to capture the multiple influences children experience in creating their gendered identity. In seeking to challenge the idea that gender identity should be tied solely to sex, Butler (1990) addresses how the multiplicity of social influences create gender identity most elegantly.

> *The presumption of a binary gender system retains the belief in a mimetic relation of gender to sex whereby gender mirrors sex or is otherwise restricted by it. When the constructed status of gender is theorized as radically independent of sex, gender itself becomes a free-floating artifice, with the consequence that* man *and* masculine *might just as easily signify a female body as a male one, and* woman *and* feminine *a male body as easily as a female body.*
>
> (Butler, 1990, p 10)

What Butler (1990) presents here is a challenge to reflect upon how as practitioners, practice can be influenced by gendered expectations that influence approaches to the care and education of children and interaction with families.

Critical question

Spend some time reflecting individually and with others on how gendered identities, such as those discussed above by Butler (1990), can influence interactions with children and families in the following situations:

» *boys and girls engaging in rough and tumble play with guns in settings;*

» *the ways girls and boys make use of the outdoor spaces in primary and secondary schools;*

» *the influence that having a predominantly female workforce within early years and primary provision might have on practice;*

» *programmes that particularly target fathers' engagement in children's learning.*

Now progress those discussions by factoring in, if you have not done so already, the role of race and class in the situations.

» *How does the addition of race and class influence the discussion?*

The discussion on '*what is childhood?*' so far has considered the social factors that shape childhoods; while not the only means, most of these factors are inevitably transmitted to children through adults who directly or indirectly inhabit their lives. Therefore, it is useful to assess in greater depth the influences adults' perspectives of childhood have in shaping the macro, meso and micro level lives of children.

Adults' perspectives of childhood

It can be said that, for adults, childhood is a universalising concept. The particulars of each adult's experience of childhood, its length and its form will vary considerably, shaped not least by those factors discussed so far in this chapter. (See Gabriel, 2010, for further discussions on adults' concepts of childhood.) Yet it remains that within adult memories there exists a concept of what childhood was, and these memories play a part in shaping ideas of what childhood is, or at least what childhood should be. However, the memories adults carry of childhood are intangible and distanced by time. Often they have become tangled by the memories of others who were there, such as parents and siblings, and while it is evidenced in the artefacts that remain, the photographs, video and objects, it is also shaped by the changes in perceptions between the child we once were and the adults we have become.

The influence of adults' memories of childhood

Yet despite these it is clear that the memories of childhood will shape the way adults approach the childhoods of the current and future generations of children, be that as parents or professionals. While the position each adult holds will vary the power they wield, that memory of childhood still holds an impact. Let us take, for example, Ban Ki-moon (Secretary General of the United Nations). He recalls a childhood shaped by colonialism from the Japanese occupation of his home, the Korean War and subsequent American involvement in South Korea that produced memories of living in hiding on a mountain side, watching towns being bombed, American soldiers throwing sweets and receiving clothes sent from America (Aldridge, 2009). These experiences alongside innumerable other personal memories will create a perspective of childhood for this man that will inevitably shape his understanding of *what childhood is*. For a person with such authority within the United Nations, this influence becomes significant.

It is worth considering how childhood experiences shape adults who are involved in the direct care and education of children. The case study below takes an interesting comparative study of pre-service teaching students that can be used to examine how the experiences they had as children shape the approach they take to the teaching of democracy. The students were from the United States and Bosnia and Herzegovina.

CASE STUDY

Lanaham, B and Phillips, M (2012) It Is Like Putting Fire in the Children's Hands: A Comparative Case Study of Pre-service Teachers' Knowledge of and Beliefs about Education for Democracy in an Established and Emerging Post-conflict Democracy. Compare: A Journal of Comparative and International Education. *September: pp 1–22*

Within this study a comparison is made regarding the beliefs pre-service teaching students have about teaching democracy. Teaching democracy within schools generally covers the teaching of government and civic rights and responsibility through problem-solving and school-based projects.

What emerged was that students from the established democracy (in this case the United States but other similar results emerged from studies with British student teachers) had often confused ideas about democracy that came from their childhood school experiences and their general lack of engagement and interest in politics and the workings of democracy. The students from the emerging postconflict democracy had a more in-depth understanding of democracy and politics, which they saw as constantly undergoing change. This reflected their childhood experiences of a country emerging from war, ethnic fighting and division.

The result was that the US students felt their education and experiences had left them unprepared to teach about democracy. The Bosnian students held far stronger views on the importance of teaching children about democracy and the dangers of its use in political violence. The Bosnian students were able to focus on the importance of rights and responsibilities and were better able to identify specific teaching strategies they could use to educate children not only about democracy and civic responsibility but also its fragility. For the US students democracy appeared to be ancient, stable and distant, and their ideas for its teaching focused on a general approach of learning to *get along together*.

For the students within this study their experiences as children had shaped the way they understood democracy and the role of citizens. These had been shaped not only by their childhood education and by the adults who had taught them but also by their personal childhood experiences that had led the US students to see democracy as a constant to be taken for granted, while the experiences of the Bosnian students was that of emerging from conflict that led them to see democracy as less stable and open to abuse.

These adults and their views had been shaped by their childhood experiences, but as student teachers they were soon to be in the role of shaping the childhood experiences of children in their care. This leads to questions regarding how students are prepared for teaching that are too broad to include here. However, it does raise interesting reflections for all adults working with children, young people and families.

Critical questions

Consider first the students in the case study.

» *What does this study tell you about how adults' childhood experiences can impact on children not only in the present but also in future generations?*

» *Compare this study with the earlier studies on African American children's understanding of race and the childhood experiences of the children of South Korean middle class mothers.*

  » *How have the adults they encounter in these studies shaped their childhoods?*

  » *How might their childhood experiences influence their understanding of childhood?*

Now consider your own practice.

» *How might your childhood experience of politics and democracy shape the way you share ideas about civil rights and responsibilities with children and young people?*

» *Reflect upon how your practice with children and young people might be shaped by your childhood experiences.*

While the impact adults have on the question *what is childhood* has been examined, it remains to be considered from the children's perspective.

Children's perspectives of childhood

There is a tendency within the adult perspectives of childhoods to position children in terms of their potential, and this risks devaluing their lived experiences. Children are frequently described in terms of human *becomings* rather than human *beings* which, even from a socially constructed stance, risks silencing the experiences of children as active agents (Waller, 2009). While the UNCRC (United Nations, 1989) has sought to empower as well as protect children and their experiences of childhood, there is still a challenge to finding how the views of children shape their childhoods. Much of the research that is included within this book has considered this challenge, and it forms part of the discussion on the impact of research on children's lives in Chapter 8. Indeed the current move within research with children reflects the contemporary focus on searching for and listening to the *voice of the child*; however, what these voices tell us and the weight they have in shaping their childhoods and that of children not yet born is inevitably subject to the influences of the social world in which they live.

The interest in children's perspectives of childhood

Smith (2010) provides an excellent critique of the ways in which children are capable of making sense of and interpreting their social worlds. From the children in Rowley et al's (2008) study of the way African American school children made sense of the impact of race upon the social interactions of adults and peers to the views of the student teachers in Lanaham and Phillip's (2012) research on what children were capable of understanding about politics, it is evident that children's opportunities to critique the social world they inhabit is subject to the power and control exhibited by adults. Nonetheless, this does not mean that within whatever space children inhabit they are not able to interpret the social forces of race, class and gender to shape and influence their own childhoods. This capacity for agency that children demonstrate has arguably always existed in some form; what has changed is the recognition and value placed upon it by adults. Childhoods and adulthoods today exist in a world that is subject to rapid changes and instability. Theories have emerged such as postmodernism and feminism that endeavour to critique the impact of globalisation, science, technology and environmental concerns upon the construction and operation of societies.

The world changes from generation to generation and so too do the ideas about what childhood is. As this chapter shows, adults have always been concerned about how best to prepare children for the world of adulthood and to provide them with the skills they consider necessary. However, the rapid changes in Western societies have led childhoods to become periods shaped by discourses of capitalism and individual rights. It is hardly surprising therefore to see that when value is placed upon the empowerment of children's individual rights, an interest emerges in research that explores how children understand and make use of these rights.

Social and cultural changes in Western societies mean that being able to utilise individual rights requires demonstrating the ability to be *flexible*. As Lee (2005) points out, *flexibility* is needed in the skills to be able to adapt to an ever-changing employment market that no longer sees adults working for one company their entire working life. This also spills into other social changes. Relationships have become open to change, with adults less likely to engage in marriage or long-term relationships and an increase in single parents and same-sex relationships. This has influenced research into how children manage social relationships and how they demonstrate agency and *flexibility*. Such studies become particularly interesting for those in charge of writing and delivering policies regarding children's education and care.

Critical questions

The way children answer the question 'what is childhood?' is seen in the research referred to throughout this book. But it is also a question worth asking children with whom you work, and having done so to consider the following.

» *What evidence is there within the answers children give of the influence of race, class and gender?*

» *What evidence do you see in the answers of children demonstrating agency in their perspectives of childhood?*

» *How do their answers differ to the answers you or your colleagues give?*

» *What adult influences are evident in the children's answers?*

The discussion of children's perspectives of childhood is inevitably influenced by the adults who inhabit their micro systems of family and social space. The influence of families and child-rearing is considered in more depth in Chapter 3.

Critical reflections

This chapter has considered some of the theoretical problems that arise when attempting to answer the question 'what is childhood?'. By critiquing the social construction of childhood, it is possible to chart how the ever-changing nature of societies and therefore childhoods make it impossible to pin any definition of childhood in time or space. It is worth reflecting, however, on the notion that the childhoods adults have experienced might influence their approaches to the childhoods of the children in their care. Adulthoods, just like childhoods, are also multiple and diverse and subject to the same influences. By recognising the role you play in shaping your experiences as an adult, you might better understand how children shape their experiences of childhood and the role you as a practitioner play in that experience.

References

Aldridge, R (2009) *Modern World Leaders: Ban Ki-Moon*. New York: Infobase Publishing.

Balagoplan, S (2002) Constructing Indigenous Childhoods: Colonialism, Vocational Education and the Working Child. *Childhood*. 9 (1): pp 19–34.

Brubaker, R (2004) *Ethnicity without Groups*. Cambridge, MA: Harvard University Press.

Butler, J (1990) *Gender Trouble: Feminism and the Subversion of Identity*. Oxon: Routledge.

Butler-Sweet, C (2011) 'Race isn't what defines me': Exploring Identity Choices in Transracial, Biracial, and Monoracial families. *Social Identities: Journal for the Study of Race, Nation and Culture*. 17 (6): pp 747–769.

Cunningham, H (2005) *Children and Childhood in Western Society since 1500*. London: Longman.

deMause, L (1974) *The Evolution of Childhood*. New York: Harper and Row.

Gabriel, N (2010) Adults' Concepts of Childhood, in Parker-Rees, R, Willan, J and Savage, J (eds) *Early Childhood Studies*, 3rd edn. Exeter: Learning Matters.

Kumar, M (2012) Introduction: Orientalism(s) after 9/11. *Journal of Postcolonial Writing*. 48 (3): pp 233–240.

Lanaham, B and Phillips, M (2012) It is Like Putting Fire in the Children's Hands: A Comparative Case Study of Pre-service Teachers' Knowledge of and Beliefs about Education for Democracy in an

Established and Emerging Post-conflict Democracy. *Compare: A Journal of Comparative and International Education*. 44 (1): pp 394–415.

Lee, N (2005) *Childhood and Society: Growing Up in an Age of Uncertainty*. Maidenhead: Open University Press.

Lowe, R (2005) Childhood through the Ages, in Maynard, T and Thomas, N (eds) *An Introduction to Early Childhood Studies*. London: Sage.

Nutbrown, C, Clough, P and Selbie, P (2009) *Early Childhood Education*. London: Sage.

Park, J and Young, I (2009) Parental Goals and Parenting Practices of Upper-Middle-Class Korean Mothers with Preschool Children. *Journal of Early Childhood Research*. 7 (1): pp 58–75.

Rowley, J, Burchinal, M, Roberts, J and Zeisel, S (2008) Racial Identity, Social Context, and Race-Related Social Cognition in African Americans During Middle Childhood. *Developmental Psychology*. 44 (6): pp 1537–1546.

Said, E (1978) *Orientalism*. London: Penguin Books.

Sanders, B (2009) Childhood in Different Cultures, in Maynard, T and Thomas, N (eds) *An Introduction to Early Childhood Studies*. London: Sage.

Smith, R (2010) *A Universal Child*. Basingstoke: Palgrave Macmillan.

Stone, D and Dolbin-MacNab, M (2013) Parent and Child Influences on the Development of a Black-White Biracial Identity. *American Psychological Association*. [online] Available at: www.apa.org/pi/families/resources/newsletter/2013/08/black-white-identity.aspx (accessed 1 February 2014).

United Nations (1989) *Convention on the Rights of the Child (UNCRC)*. New York: United Nations.

Waller, T (2009) Modern Childhood: Contemporary Theories and Children's Lives, in Waller, T (ed) *An Introduction to Early Childhood*. London: Sage.

Wells, K (2009) *Childhood in a Global Perspective*. Cambridge: Polity.

3 Families and parenting

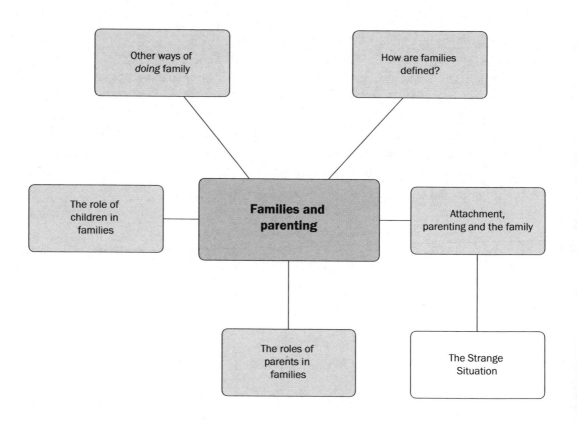

They need loving families, where they observe and experience love, and thus learn how to love others. They also need boundaries to be set by parents who are firm but not dictatorial.

(Layard and Dunn, 2009, p 10)

Introduction

This chapter examines the way social values shape and control families and parenting. The influence these values have range from the roles individual members play within the family to the ways parents control and protect their children. Examining these values from a global perspective reveals the extent to which they impact upon the diverse experiences children have of family and parenting.

This chapter is divided into five parts:

1. how are families defined?

2. other ways of *doing* family;

3. attachment theory and the family;

4. the roles of parents in families;

5. the role of children in families.

The quote at the start of the chapter positions the family as the place best able to meet a child's needs. This wisdom has been built into societies over generations and with it have grown the innumerable ideas and values of how this is best achieved. If we examine the principles behind this quote then questions begin to form which support an analysis of the role families play in shaping childhoods.

Critical questions

» *How do we recognise what a loving family looks like?*

» *How might the loving actions children observe and experience shape their interactions with others?*

» *What is meant by the term boundaries in relation to children, and who/what might influence a judgement on the boundaries' correct placement?*

» *How might socially constructed values influence the point at which firm becomes dictatorial?*

How are families defined?

Just as Chapter 2 analysed how society shapes childhood, so too a study of the impact families have on childhoods reveals social norms and expectations. Contemporary Western studies argue that the family, once viewed as a private space, has increasingly become the focus of research and state interventions (Robinson and Diaz, 2006) across the world. Yet the influence societies have upon the nature and function of families has always been integral to shaping the changes in families over time.

The rise in dominance of the nuclear family is frequently credited to the introduction of industrialisation. The movement of peasants from the rural norms of the countryside to the newly emerging industrial cities brought changes to the size and function of the family unit (Shorter, 1977); extended families composed of several generations living together gave way to the smaller, more flexible nuclear family. The nuclear family, lacking the ties of extended relatives, came to represent the neoliberal *ideals* of independence and mobility, able to meet the requirements of the modern state. Indeed the influence of this Western ideal remains today and can be seen in the United Nations Statistics Division (2013) definition of a family nucleus:

A family nucleus is one of the following types (each of which must consist of persons living in the same household):

- *A married couple without children*

- *A married couple with one or more unmarried children*

- *A father with one or more unmarried children*

- *A mother with one or more unmarried children*

- *Couples living in consensual unions should be regarded as married couples.*

(United Nations Statistics Division, 2013)

This is in contrast to the definition of extended families which the United Nations define as *extended households*:

Extended household, defined as a household consisting of any one of the following:

- *A single family nucleus and other persons related to the nucleus, for example, a father with child(ren) and other relative(s) or a married couple with other relative(s) only*

- *Two or more family nuclei related to each other without any other persons, for example, two or more married couples with child(ren) only*

- *Two or more family nuclei related to each other plus other persons related to at least one of the nuclei, for example, two or more married couples with other relative(s) only*

- *Two or more persons related to each other, none of whom constitute a family nucleus*

(United Nations Statistics Division, 2013)

Indeed the United Nations define a third type of family/household – the composite households:

Composite household, defined as a household consisting of any of the following:

- *A single family nucleus plus other persons, some of whom are related to the nucleus and some of whom are not, for example, mother with child(ren) and other relatives and nonrelatives*

- *A single family nucleus plus other persons, none of whom is related to the nucleus, for example, father with child(ren) and nonrelatives*

- *Two or more family nuclei related to each other plus other persons, some of whom are related to at least one of the nuclei and some of whom are not related to any of the nuclei, for example, two or more couples with other relatives and nonrelatives only*

- *Two or more family nuclei related to each other plus other persons, none of whom is related to any of the nuclei, for example, two or more married couples one or more of which with child(ren) and non-relatives*

- *Two or more family nuclei not related to each other, with or without any other persons*

- *Two or more persons related to each other but none of whom constitute a family nucleus, plus other unrelated persons*

- *Non-related persons only*

(United Nations Statistics Division, 2013)

A final category is marked as *other/unknown* (United Nations Statistics Division, 2013).

The influence the macro level state has in shaping and defining these families can be seen in actions across the world. From communist Russian and Chinese state policies aimed at controlling both the size and function of families (Brassard and Chen, 2005) to Germany's historical use of family policies to promote the function of a particular middle class nuclear family, which discouraged mothers from working (Bühler-Niederberger, 2003), states used, and continue to use, policies to shape families. What becomes apparent is the extent to which the family, like childhood, as a social construct is subject to change and multiplicity.

As the universal child no longer exists, so the same can be said of a universal family in which that child resides. Families emerge as contested spaces that reflect the *heat* from the values held by the societies in which they sit. This is increasingly evident in the twenty-first century as societies globally become subject to rapid changes with families frequently becoming the spaces in which these changes are most divisive. Social changes such as gendered and transgendered roles in society, economic instability and population migration have all come to define the multiplicity of families globally. Families are no longer restricted within nation-states but have become subject to transnational changes. '*These forces have the potential to advance and empower or exploit and oppress families and their members, as well as whole societies*' (Wilkes Karraker, 2013, p 11).

Critical questions

Reflect upon your family and the families of children with whom you work, and use the discussions above to consider the following questions.

» *What significance does the term* household *rather than* family *have for the United Nations' definitions?*

»   *Analyse ways in which political policies on education, welfare, immigration and legislation normalise nuclear families in the United Kingdom?*

»   *What conclusions might we draw regarding the potential these forces have to advance and empower or exploit and oppress families and their members?*

If there is no universal family it is worth considering the different approaches to families and the impact these have upon children in more depth.

Other ways of *doing* family

The impact of social changes on families in the past 30 years has been dramatic. Statistics from the OECD (2011) report the following.

- More women are in employment with an increase in families where both parents work, although women, on average, earn less than men.

- Fewer children are being born, leading to a rise in population age and smaller families.

- Couples are postponing having children, meaning women are older when they have children (OECD average age 28 years).

- There is a decrease in marriage and a rise in divorces (although marriage remains the most common form of partnership).

- There has been an increase in sole parent and *reconstituted families*, with the number of sole parents expected to rise the most in future.

- There is an increase in child poverty in sole parent families.

However, these are not the only changes that have occurred within societies. The rise in same-sex families has meant that in the United States alone an estimated 6 million children and adults have lesbian, gay, bisexual or transgender (LGBT) parents (Gates, 2013). At times these families have given rise to contentious discussions about social and religious ideas on parenting and demonstrate the *Othering* that families can experience and the challenges for children growing up in families whose values are questioned. While there is much heated discussion that tends to circulate around a *what-is-best-for-the-child* style debate, the voices of the children central to this are heard less often. In a study relevant to this debate, 14 American adolescents aged between 13 and 18, 2 males and 12 females, from same-sex parent families discuss their identities as part of families, peer groups and wider American society.

CASE STUDY

Welsh, G (2011) *Growing Up in a Same-Sex Parented Family: The Adolescent Voice of Experience.* Journal of GLBT Family Studies. *7 (1–2): pp 49–71.*

In this study children spoke of times when they were made to feel less valued because of their family and experiences of their families being described as *abnormal*. While many believed that marriage between same-sex couples should be a civil right, they did not see this as a means of legitimising their families, but rather a way of speeding up tolerance within wider society. When the children discussed developing their own sense of identity they described complex, and at times difficult, feelings and experiences. They showed a wish to distance themselves from their parents' sexual orientation in order to gain a sense of their own unique qualities and characteristics that did not limit them to stereotypes about their family. Although negotiating multiple identities and social situations at times led them to feel a sense of loss or betrayal of their prominent family identity, many felt they had gained resilience and a deeper understanding of diversity.

However, this did not make them immune to difficult times, particularly at the start of puberty when early encounters with homophobia meant they had often tried to shield their parents from worry or unhappiness. The children described using strategies to hide their family's true identity that had to sit with a strong sense of family loyalty; however, some also warned against becoming a *poster child* for same-sex families that would mean they failed to reflect on their own lives honestly. When the children did disclose their family structure to friends it was often with a sense of anxiety over trust. Having support from children who were also from same-sex families had offered the children the opportunity to share their experiences with others who could understand.

Welsh concludes that the messages from government, the media and society about what it meant to have gay parents meant that children of same-sex parents had to negotiate and reconcile these ideas with their own identities. While early puberty was a particularly difficult time, there remained a desire for society to understand the benefits of having gay parents. The most striking thought to emerge from the study was the importance the children placed on being able to live lives that would not be held in simplified comparisons with heterosexual families, which would deny the existence and power of the challenges they face.

Welsh highlights the importance of those working with children being conscious of the messages that their settings convey about same-sex families, through both what is said and what is not said. Understanding the unique needs of individual children and families reduces the risk of stereotyping and creates a sense of empowerment for the children through a secure and stable space where children can reflect and share their thoughts safely.

Critical questions

After reading the case study, consider the following questions.

» *What is the relationship between macro level ideas about family and the micro level experiences of these children?*

» *What is your opinion of the concern some children expressed of being a poster child for same-sex families? Justify this response.*

» *Reflect upon your practice and consider how you could improve the care of children from same-sex families?*

»   *Reflect upon your setting and consider what changes could be made to create safe and stable space for children to reflect and share their thoughts honestly?*

Analysing other ways of doing family extends far beyond same-sex families to include single parents, extended families and child-headed households; a common theme raised in these discussions is that of attachment theory.

Attachment, parenting and the family

The theory of attachment as formulated by John Bowlby (1907–90) has had a profound influence upon parents, institutions and childcare experts in the West since it first came to prominence in postwar Britain. In brief, the theory promotes an evolutionary, biological aspect to the mother/caregiver bond with the infant child. The child's survival depends upon this bond and so young children have developed a universal characteristic set of behaviours (such as crying and smiling) in order to maintain a close proximity to the mother, particularly at times of stress. Importantly, the mother's response to these stimuli results in the child becoming either securely or insecurely attached. The theory maintains that the effect of this attachment on the child impacts beyond childhood and into adult life.

Attachment theory has influenced the care of children in hospitals and childcare institutions internationally. In 1952 Bowlby presented a report to the World Health Organization, '*Maternal Care and Mental Health*', in which he linked children's attachment to, primarily, their mothers with their mental health in adulthood. It is interesting to read the opinions towards families and parenting held in this period. Descriptions of young mothers of illegitimate children as *irrational* or *neurotic* (Bowlby, 1952, pp 93, 94) reflect a view that saw unmarried mothers as unlikely to be effective carers for their children. This undoubtedly influenced the approaches governments in the United Kingdom and other Western nations took that advocated the adoption of these babies as soon as possible after birth.

While the basic premise of attachment carries recognition of the importance of early and secure relationships for young children, much of Bowlby's theories have been critiqued in recent times; the most significant being the emphasis Bowlby placed on a hierarchy of relationships, particularly the prominence given to the primary and unique role of the mother (monotropy). Building on this, *maternal deprivation* was the term Bowlby used if there was separation, loss or failure to develop an attachment to the mother; this Bowlby argued caused harm to a child that persisted into adulthood. This was later challenged on several points. Rutter (1981) contended that this was an oversimplification, and instead defined *maternal deprivation* as the complete loss of the maternal attachment. He proposed that a failure to develop an attachment was in fact *privation* which was potentially more serious. Hodges and Tizard (1989) countered that while early and secure attachments were important, the damage from deprivation or privation could be reversed through loving care later in childhood. Indeed finding direct correlations between either maternal deprivation or privation and problems in adulthood is difficult when the impact of other wider social experiences a child has might also be a factor.

The Strange Situation

Another aspect of monotropy is the principle of secure attachment to the primary caregiver/ mother figure. Using the Strange Situation (Ainsworth et al, 1978), Mary Ainsworth, a colleague of Bowlby, presented a test to measure how securely young children are attached to their primary caregiver. (See Posada's (2008) detailed discussion on attachment, the work of Bowlby, Ainsworth and the Strange Situation). The test was devised using American children and their mothers. Ainsworth et al (1978) monitored the children's responses to being reunited with their mother after being left with a stranger for a short time. From their responses, the children were placed within three general categories.

1. Secure attachment – explored with their mother present, became distressed when mother left but settled on her return.

2. Anxious insecure attachment (anxious resistant) – remained clinging to mother and became overly distressed when left, taking longer to settle.

3. Avoidant insecure attachment (anxious avoidant) – appeared *detached* and indifferent to the mother's presence and appeared not to recognise mother on reunion.

The responses were used to categorise levels of secure and insecure attachment between mother and child. Yet, when conducted in different countries (Cole, 1998), cultural variances emerged. Japanese and Israeli children demonstrated similar levels of secure attachment to American children; however, less American children demonstrated anxious insecure attachment, whilst children in Northern Germany demonstrated less secure attachment and greater anxious avoidant attachment. If Cole's (1998) analysis suggests that the different responses of these children to the Strange Situation means that the test produces transferable, standardised results (which had been the case in its application to minority groups in the United States), then a high number of Japanese children demonstrated an anxious-resistant state. Either these children were insecurely attached to their mothers or they found the Strange Situation more stressful and became particularly upset when their mothers left. (See Further Reading for sources on the Strange Situation and attachment.)

However, Klebanov and Travis (2015) contend that the study of brain development upholds the theory that early insecure attachments can have serious physical and psychological impacts upon children, arguing that even *minimal* neglectful child-rearing can result in disordered behaviours which impair mental development and future mental health. Certainly during the first three years of life the brain's plasticity does make it uniquely susceptible to environmental factors. This suggests not only that early brain development influences children's and adults' coping mechanisms but also that the brain becomes *encultured* (Downey and Lende, 2012) by the social and cultural values it experiences in early childhood.

The debate on whether children's responses to the Strange Situation reflect their cultural experiences or behaviours demonstrating secure or insecure attachment will no doubt continue. However, four points remain.

1. The existence of a universal element to attachment theory linked to biological responses.

2. The early years of a child's life are a particularly influential period for brain development.

3. The premise that problems in adulthood linked to insecure attachment are a focus of much study.

4. The aspects that appear to have a cultural element are complex and need to be explored further.

Critical questions

Consider the role of attachment theory on your practice with children and families.

»   *In your opinion, what does Bowlby's monotropy theory suggest about broader social values? Justify your answer.*

»   *Having researched attachment theory what do you think are the features of a child's experience of maternal privation that could impact on them in later childhood or as adults?*

»   *What elements of attachment theory would you classify as culturally specific? How would you support that view?*

Attachment theory demonstrates the important role parents play in meeting the needs of children for security and protection.

The roles of parents in families

The historical and cultural experiences of childhood as discussed in Chapter 2 are inextricably bound with the ways parents view their roles. Certainly the discussion on attachment theory reflects how the focus on parents, and mothers in particular, has emerged out of the mid-twentieth century.

The role of parents in meeting the care needs of children, especially young children, may have universal qualities such as those identified by Maslow's (1954) hierarchy of needs; yet these are also argued to be subject to cultural influences. For example, Super and Harkness (1998) examined how the universal elements of emotional development, as explained through Bowlby's theory of attachment, meant that *separation anxiety* and *fear of strangers* are influenced by the culture in which the children are raised. Reflecting on the comparisons that Cole (1998) made, Super and Harkness (1998) compared parenting in America with that of the Kipsigis tribe of western Kenya. The conclusions suggest that it is in the culturally specific ways in which parents raise their children that the universal elements of Maslow's needs become differentiated. American parents took their children into wider society, meaning they experienced strangers more often than Kipsigis children; this made American children less likely to be fearful of strangers. However, Kipsigis mothers kept their children in almost constant physical contact with them for the first four months after which they were raised within extended families of carers, unlike American children who were raised in smaller nuclear families with less physical contact. The Kipsigis children showed less separation anxiety than their American peers. Super and Harkness concluded that the cultural differences in the children's development resulted from the values of their parents about the *correct* way to raise their children.

Parental values are influenced by broader socio-cultural ideas that become embedded in the way parents view their role. It is worth pausing to consider what these socio-cultural ideas are and how they influence the values that parents develop. Throughout this book the influence of cultural ideas of race, class and gender on children's lives has been shown as important, and one of the most powerful ways these cultural ideas are transmitted into children's lives is within the family via the parents. Numerous studies (see Chapter 2 for Park and Young's study of South Korean upper middle class mothers and Chapter 7 for Yeo's study of bonding and attachment in Australian Aboriginal children) have produced cross-cultural comparisons on how parents transmit the wider socio-cultural values of the community. Japanese parents, for example, have been shown to value consideration of other people and civic responsibility more highly than US parents who are more likely to value a sense of fairness and creativity (Naito and Gielen, 2005). These parental values form an important link in the way parenting supports children's socialisation.

The role of the state in mediating the social values of *good* parents has gained prominence. Western governments seeking to manage fiscal problems have increasingly used the rhetoric of *troubled families* to make welfare expenditure a means with which to regulate *poor parenting* (Jensen, 2013) and promote a view of idealised parental behaviour.

Critical questions

Consider how parental values in families with whom you work transmit broader socio-cultural ideas.

» How might parents transmit wider social views about gender roles to their children?

» Why is it important for practitioners to understand the influence parental values have on children as they grow and develop?

» Evaluate the contribution parental values might make to children developing secure attachments.

» In your opinion, how influential are government policies, the media or you as a practitioner in shaping parental behaviour?

The common means of describing the process by which parental values are transmitted to children is *parenting styles*. Parenting styles are frequently categorised using Diana Baumrind's (Baumrind, 1967) descriptors:

• authoritative (often identified as both responsive and demanding);

• authoritarian (often identified as less responsive and more demanding);

• permissive (often identified as more responsive and less demanding).

From a Western perspective, authoritative parenting style is generally considered the most beneficial to children's well-being with its reciprocal dialogue between parents and children. Engagement with digital technology presents an interesting area for examining parenting styles. In their study, Correa et al (2013) conclude that new technologies offer a reversal of roles as children, often referred to as *digital natives* (Prensky, 2001), influence parents' engagement with new technologies. The study found children's power particularly noticeable in low socio-economic families where technology in the home was less common, and for women in the family who may be less likely to engage with the technology and be more open to support from their children. However, the influence of parenting styles persists when managing the way children use digital technology once they have accessed the internet. The study below examines the attitudes of Italian parents to children's use of mobile internet technology and the way parenting styles are used to manage their children's engagement in the technology.

CASE STUDY

Mascheroni, G (2013) Parenting the Mobile Internet in Italian Households: Parents' and Children's Discourses. Journal of Children and Media. *Published online 2 September 2013.*

In this study the influence of parenting styles on parents' mediation of their children's mobile internet technology is examined through focus group discussions. Three discussions were conducted with parents of children aged 10–13 years of age and one was conducted with children from the same age group. Links emerge between parenting styles, the parents' relationships with their children and parental attitudes to information and communication technology (ICT).

From the study, the decision to provide their children with smartphones was gendered, with fathers identifying opportunities to engage with personal media, while mothers legitimised ownership with remote parenting and co-ordinating family life. Fathers reported higher self-efficacy with digital technology than mothers; yet mothers particularly expressed fear that their children's lack of experience and critical skills made them vulnerable to inappropriate content and contact, with parents perceiving daughters as being at greater risk than sons. The parents were concerned that while mobile phones could be legitimised for maintaining family communication, smartphones were a means for their children to evade parental monitoring and pursue activities they felt required more control, a view which the children disagreed with.

Most parents tended to adopt authoritative or permissive parenting styles when regulating their children's use of the technology. Parents expected children to internalise the values of the parents which arguably supports the social view of *good parenting* being reflected in the authoritative parenting style.

However, for some parents more authoritarian parenting styles were favoured; six parents favoured a more controlling approach. For the mothers who took this approach, lower digital literacy appeared to result in a preference for monitoring and restricting access, while the fathers who favoured this approach defined this more in terms of their wider approach to managing family patterns rather than a lack of expertise in ICT.

For the authoritative and permissive parents, there tended to be active engagement in their children's use of the technology. Parents often guided their children's use of the technology, seeing this as a way of promoting responsible use and to legitimise their own surveillance of their children's engagement with social media as a way to protect them from negative online experiences. The parents spoke of the importance of discussing risk awareness and coping strategies with their children. While authoritarian parents reported monitoring their children's activities using approaches such as checking their children's computer and smartphone history periodically, authoritative parents tended to monitor use by restricting their children's engagement with technology to certain times or through *pay as you go* to restrict internet use.

The children were not passive recipients of their parents' mediation; Mascheroni reports how the children negotiate, resist and ignore their parents' attempts at regulating their use of the technology. Ignoring attempts by parents to *friend* them on Facebook and selecting privacy settings that exclude parents from online conversations were two common approaches by children.

What emerged is a tension around the role of mobile technology and the way parents approach their children's engagement with it. For parents the technology offers an opportunity for children to have responsibilities while maintaining perpetual contact with them. For children the technology offers freedom from parental surveillance while providing a sense of security from keeping contact with parents.

This study reveals the dominance of authoritative parenting styles in Western ideas of *good parenting*. However, this view is not universal. Keshavarz and Baharudin (2009) contend that parenting styles have a cultural significance based on the wider context in which they are used, arguing that in collectivist societies authoritarian parenting styles can be seen as caring and concerned parenting, unlike the controlling and dictatorial perception it holds in Western ideas. With this in mind use the questions below to reflect upon the case study.

Critical questions

» *How would you assess the role gender played in the parenting styles that parents engaged in?*

» *What conclusions might we draw regarding the cultural context of both the parenting styles of the parents and the responses of the children?*

» *What alternative non-Western views might societies hold of* good parenting? *See the case study in Chapter 2 regarding South Korean mothers (Park and Young, 2009).*

» *How does this case study compare with your practice/experience?*

While the role of parents is obviously crucial to the experiences children have of family life, what can be seen from the Italian case study is that children are not passive within the family dynamic. The parenting styles employed are important influences on family dynamics yet they are not the sole factor; children as active agents within the family also requires further examination.

The role of children in families

If the family is the space in which children first come to learn about wider social structures such as identity and roles, Mascheroni's (2013) study shows children are also active in understanding and negotiating their position within the family. Western ideas of family and childhood may focus on the protection of children's innocence yet this combines with *teaching* children the social norms inevitably required for children to navigate the society in which they live. As with many areas in Western culture, the Italian parents in Mascheroni's (2013) study agonised over *giving* control and power to children in a way that would keep them safe in the complex world of internet communication. Many of these concerns can be translated into other areas of modern life within industrialised nations, such as fear over road safety, crime and strangers, that stop children playing on the streets outside their home, or the risk of injury that limits children's experiences of managing risk in their play. Parenting styles arguably reflect not only the role factors such as these play in societies but also the social and cultural responses families will have.

While children actively create and negotiate their own roles and positions within the family, for some children the concept of agency contrasts sharply to the experiences of the children in Italy. The concept of the child-headed household (CHH) has become a phenomenon inextricably linked to the HIV/AIDS pandemic across sub-Saharan Africa. While the figures for the number of children who have been orphaned by the disease and how many are living within a CHH is contested (Meintjes and Giese, 2006), what is seen is that across this region there are children who experience a family in which there is no significant adult presence. The way this family structure impacts upon the children is explored in the study detailed below conducted in Zimbabwe. In Zimbabwe, as in many nations across Africa, the colonisation and postcolonial political upheaval disrupted traditional social means of caring for children who lose their parents. (See Chapter 7 for a discussion on postcolonisation theory.) The arrival of HIV exacerbated this problem further, with the emergence of families with no permanent adult and headed by older siblings.

CASE STUDY

Francis-Chizororo, M (2010) Growing Up Without Parents: Socialisation and Gender Relations in Orphaned-Child-Headed Households in Rural Zimbabwe. Journal of Southern African Studies. *36 (3): pp 711–727.*

This ethnographic study was conducted with five CHHs from five villages across the rural district of Mashonaland West Province, Zimbabwe; the children ranged in age from 10 to 19 years of age. Age was the most important feature to being the head in the CHH, reflecting the cultural generational hierarchy within the society, but this position was continually contested and was also dependant on the ability to bring food into the household. Elder girls might not see themselves as the head of the family despite fulfilling that function.

The elder children did not consider themselves as a mother or father for their younger siblings, instead describing their roles as providing food, giving advice as an aunt or uncle might, making decisions, participating in community activities, distributing household chores, paid work and supporting other siblings living with relatives elsewhere. Although they did not use the terms mother and father, gendered roles were still maintained. At times this led to conflict between the children as, for example, older boys tried to exercise control over the adolescent girls in a bid to protect them from boys.

Similarly, household chores were also influenced by gender identity. All the children contributed to the household chores, despite these traditionally being seen as female roles; boys were required to participate particularly in all male households. In households with both boys and girls there were tasks that the boys were not prepared to do such as washing dishes and sweeping the yard, while they were willing to cook. The boys felt conscious of being *laughed at* by their friends if they were seen washing dishes outside the home or sweeping. The risk of being denied food for not assisting was seen as relevant for compliance with chores. All siblings were involved in some kind of paid work, with younger children using money raised from paid jobs within the villages to meet personal needs such as school uniforms while the child heads would travel further to earn money to provide food for the family.

Francis-Chizororo concludes that, like adult-headed households, CHHs are kinship units characterised as places for decision-making and socialisation where power structures and gendered roles are negotiated.

The experiences of the children within the CHHs demonstrate not only the breadth of child-hood experiences but also the agency children are capable of when faced with such challenging situations. The family unit the children replicate mirrors the social and cultural families of their communities. Use the questions below to critically analyse the experiences of the children in the CHHs that Francis-Chizororo studied.

Critical questions

»   *How have macro level ideas about family impacted upon the micro level experiences of these children? Compare your answer to the one given for the Welsh (2011) study at the start of this chapter.*

»   *How might the experiences of the children in this study be analysed in terms of attachment theory?*

»   *What do CHHs tell you about different ways of doing family?*

»   *How do the experiences of these children inform your ideas about children's agency and children's rights?*

It is unsurprising that children living in the most challenging situations are often called upon to demonstrate the greatest level of agency. Yet the studies in this chapter have demonstrated that internationally children are actively involved in demonstrating their agency within families. This might be restricted and managed by parents and the wider society in which they live but it is nevertheless apparent.

Critical reflections

This chapter has considered some of the ways that families influence experiences of childhood. The way that societies construct values around the ideal family and good parenting continue to change. These can cause tensions when families differ significantly from those the wider society might idealise. The notion of the nuclear family has become significant in Western societies and has led to problems for those whose families do not reflect that idea of a family, be that in the context of single parent, same-sex parents or extended families. The child-headed household offers an additional way of doing family rarely seen in Western societies.

Similarly the notion of parenting and what style of parenting constitutes *good* suggests that the dominance of Western views can be challenged when seen through the cultural lens of different societies. A *good parent* might have some universal qualities but these are subject to the social values that shape the family in which the parenting is enacted.

As Western ideas become more widespread through global communications and organisations such as the United Nations, it is important to recognise the different ideas of families and the significance they have in the lives of children.

By analysing these ideas of families and parenting, the social construction of childhood can be seen in clearer contexts. It is worth reflecting upon how your ideas of parenting and family might impact on the way you work with children and families.

Further reading

Attachment theory and the Strange Situation are explored in: Prior, V and Glaser, D (2006) *Understanding Attachment and Attachment Disorders. Theory, Evidence and Practice.* London: Jessica Kingsley Publisher.

The role of parenting in children's development is examined in: Klebanov, M and Travis, A (2015) *The Critical Role of Parenting in Human Development.* London: Routledge.

References

Ainsworth, M, Blehar, M, Waters, E and Wall, S (1978) *Patterns of Attachment: A Psychological Study of the Strange Situation.* Hillsdale, NJ: Unwin Hyman.

Baumrind, D (1967) Child-Care Practices Anteceding Three Patterns of Preschool Behavior. *Genetic Psychology Monographs.* 75 (1): pp 43–88.

Bowlby, J (1952) *Mental Care and Mental Health.* Geneva: World Health Organization. WHO, Institutional Repository for Information Sharing. [online] Available at: http://apps.who.int/iris/handle/10665/40724 (accessed 13 April 2014).

Brassard, M and Chen, S (2005) Boarding of Upper Middle Class Toddlers in China. *Psychology in the Schools*. 42 (3): pp 297–304.

Bühler-Niederberger, D (2003) The Needy Child and the Naturalisation of Politics. Political Debate in Germany, in Hallett, C and Prout, A (eds) *Hearing the Voices of Children*. Abingdon: Routledge Falmer.

Cole, M (1998) Culture in Development, in Woodhead, M, Faulkner, D and Littleton, K (eds) *Cultural Worlds of Early Childhood*. Oxon: Routledge.

Correa, T, Straubhaar, J, Chen, W and Spence, J (2013) Brokering New Technologies: The Role of Children in Their Parents' Usage of the Internet. *New Media Society*. 0(0) : pp 1–18

Downey, G and Lende, D (2012) Neuroanthrapology and the Encultured Brain, in Lende, D and Downey, G (eds) *The Encultured Brain*. Massachusetts: MIT.

Francis-Chizororo, M (2010) Growing Up without Parents: Socialisation and Gender Relations in Orphaned-Child-Headed Households in Rural Zimbabwe. *Journal of Southern African Studies*. 36 (3): pp 711–727.

Gates, G (2013) LGBT Parenting in the United States. [online] Available at: http://williamsinstitute. law.ucla.edu/research/census-lgbt-demographics-studies/lgbt-parenting-in-the-united-states/ (accessed 11 April 2014).

Hodges, J and Tizard, B (1989) Social and Family Relationships of Ex-Institutional Adolescents. *Journal of Child Psychology and Psychiatry*. 30 (1): pp 77–97.

Jensen, T (2013) Austerity Parenting: Narratives of Austerity Are Central to an Agenda That Seeks to Link Poverty with Fecklessness. *Soundings*. 55: pp 60–70.

Keshavarz, S and Baharudin, R (2009) Parenting Style in a Collectivist Culture of Malaysia. *European Journal of Social Science*. 10 (1): pp 66–73.

Klebanov, M and Travis, A (2015) *The Critical Role of Parenting in Human Development*. London: Routledge.

Layard, R and Dunn, J (2009) *A Good Childhood: Searching for Values in a Competitive Age*. London: Penguin Books.

Mascheroni, G (2013) Parenting the Mobile Internet in Italian Households: Parents' and Children's Discourses. *Journal of Children and Media*. Published online 2 September 2013.

Maslow, A H (1954) *Motivation and Personality*. New York: Harper and Row.

Meintjes, H and Giese, S (2006) Spinning the Epidemic: The Making of Mythologies of Orphanhood in the Context of AIDS. *Childhood*. 13 (3): pp 407–430.

Naito, T and Gielen, U (2005) The Changing Japanese Family: A Psychological Portrait, in Roopnarine, J L and Gielen, U (eds) *Families in Global Perspectives*. Boston: Pearson.

OECD (2011) *Doing Better for Families*. Paris: OECD Publishing.

Park, J and Young, I (2009) Parental Goals and Parenting Practices of Upper-Middle-Class Korean Mothers with Preschool Children. *Journal of Early Childhood Research*. 7 (1): pp 58–75.

Posada, G (2008) Attachment, in Benson, J and Marshall, M (eds) *Social and Emotional Development in Infancy and Early Childhood*. Oxford: Academic Press.

Prensky, M (2001) Digital Natives, Digital Immigrants. *On the Horizon*. 9: pp 1–6.

Robinson, K H and Diaz, C J (2006) *Diversity and Difference in Early Childhood Education: Issues for Theory and Practice.* Maidenhead: Open University Press.

Rutter, M (1981) *Maternal Deprivation Reassessed.* London: Penguin Books.

Shorter, E (1977) *The Making of the Modern Family.* New York: Basic Books.

Super, C M and Harkness, S (1998) The Development of Affect in Infancy and Early Childhood, in Woodhead, M, Faulkner, D and Littletop, K (eds) *Cultural Worlds of Early Childhood.* London: Routledge.

United Nations Statistics Division (2013) Households and Families. [online] Available at: http://unstats. un.org/unsd/demographic/sconcerns/fam/fammethods.htm#A2 (accessed 10 April 2014).

Welsh, G (2011) Growing Up in a Same-Sex Parented Family: The Adolescent Voice of Experience. *Journal of GLBT Family Studies.* 7 (1–2): pp 49–71.

Wilkes Karraker, M (2013) *Global Families,* 2nd edn. London: Sage.

4 International views on education

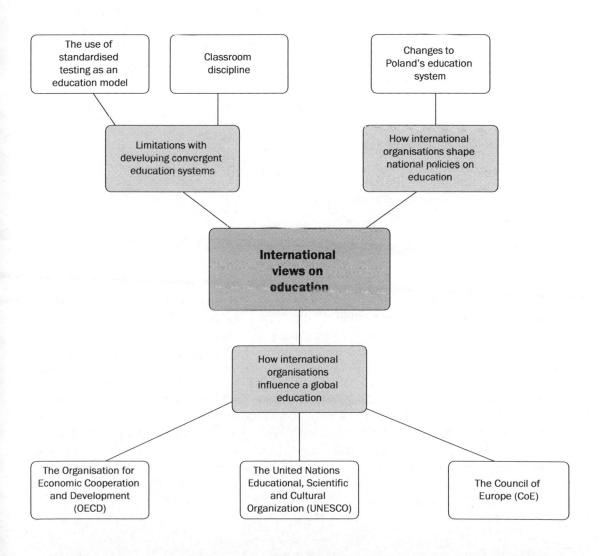

Education has become a commodity with both the individual and the state as consumer, the individual seeking to maximise personal benefit and the state seeking to maximise economic growth and development. ... the implication of this is that the most effective route to economic well-being for any society is through the development of the skills of its population, its human capital. Consequently, education is to be regarded as a productive investment rather than merely a form of consumption or something intrinsically valuable in its own right.

(Bell and Stevenson, 2006, p 46)

Introduction

This chapter takes an international perspective on how education impacts upon the lives of children. As the quote by Bell and Stevenson (2006) demonstrates, education has become one of the most powerful tools a nation has to develop children's individual intellectual skills, shape them into national citizens and prepare them to become workers in a global economy. The approaches individual nations take to achieve these might differ, but this chapter demonstrates how the drive to use education to achieve *economic well-being* in a global economy means individual nations are increasingly part of converging international education systems that shape global childhoods. Consequently it is important for those who work with children, whether in education or not, to understand and reflect upon what these international systems are, how they influence national approaches to education, and some of the associated problems.

This chapter is divided into three parts:

1. how international organisations influence a global education;

2. how international organisations shape national policies on education;

3. limitations with developing convergent education systems.

The first part considers the impact international organisations have on the education of children. Three major organisations are examined – the United Nations Educational, Scientific and Cultural Organization (UNESCO), the Organisation for Economic Cooperation and Development (OECD) and the Council of Europe (CoE). These organisations have become hugely influential in the creation of individual national education systems and are helping to create a convergence in education internationally. For example, the coordinated approach the CoE, supported by UNESCO, is seeking to improve the education of children from the Roma community across Europe.

The second part considers two examples of how social and political changes as well as international organisations impact upon the education of children within nations. First it will analyse changes the Polish education system has undergone in the past 25 years, as it passed from a communist nation to a democratic nation. This moves on to consider the professionalising of the early childhood education and care workforce and the influence international organisations have on the approaches taken by individual nations, particularly regarding the separation of education and care.

The third part of this chapter examines the problems and challenges of developing convergent education systems. The role standardised testing plays in the development of these systems and as a means of evaluating the quality of children's education is explored. The pressures that can result from standardised testing combined with the convergence of education systems by nations with diverse cultural and social values means classroom discipline has become an area of much debate. The challenges of recognising different approaches to classroom discipline within convergent education systems are also examined.

Critical questions

The quote at the start of the chapter suggests that education has become a means by which individuals and nations seek to achieve economic well-being. The result is a shift in perception, which means education has become an investment commodity rather than something to be consumed or valued in its own right.

»   *How does this view of education benefit children?*

»   *How does this view limit children's education?*

»   *What does this view of education say about how ideas regarding childhoods are developing?*

»   *What is your opinion of education as 'something intrinsically valuable in its own right'?*

How international organisations influence a global education

On a macro level, international education systems are closely linked to the human rights agenda (see Chapter 5) and the global economy. Three international organisations with significant influence upon global perspectives of education are: the UNESCO, the OECD and the CoE (as defined in the introduction).

The United Nations Educational, Scientific and Cultural Organization (UNESCO)

In 1945 UNESCO's constitution cited its aims as '... *to contribute to peace and security by promoting collaboration among the nations through education, science and culture in order to further universal respect for justice, for the rule of law and for the human rights and fundamental freedoms which are affirmed for the peoples of the world*' (UNESCO, 1945). UNESCO has 195 member states and manages a commitment to education through its co-ordination of the movement Education for All (EfA) (see Further Reading). Working with United Nations Children's Fund (UNICEF) and the World Bank, it has six educational goals.

•   Goal 1: to expand and improve comprehensive early childhood care and education, particularly for the most vulnerable and disadvantaged children.

- Goal 2: to ensure that by 2015 all children have access to complete, free and compulsory primary education, particularly for girls and children from ethnic minorities.

- Goal 3: to ensure the learning needs of all young people are met through equitable access to appropriate learning and life skills programmes.

- Goal 4: to achieve 50 per cent improvement in levels of adult literacy by 2015, particularly for women.

- Goal 5: to eliminate gender disparities in primary and secondary education and achieve gender equality by 2015.

- Goal 6: to improve all aspects of the quality of education and ensuring excellence to achieve measurable learning outcomes particularly in literacy, numeracy and essential life skills.

Education for All also supports two educational elements of the Millennium Development Goals (UN, 2014), all with the deadline of 2015 (see Chapter 6). The EfA's annual report in 2014 (UNESCO, 2014) identified that while progress has been made towards addressing goals of universal education and eliminating inequality, none of the goals it set will be met globally by 2015.

A key issue leading to the failure to meet these goals is the funding of education. The EfA report highlights how reduced spending on education by governments in low and middle income nations, combined with a reduction in aid from higher income nations, has contributed to the failure to meet the educational goals (UNESCO, 2014, p 111). While a number of governments in low and middle income nations, such as Afghanistan, Benin and Ethiopia, have increased their spending on children's education, international targets on government investment in education have never been set. As many of these nations, such as India, are now experiencing growth in their economies, UNESCO is arguing for governments to use tax-raising powers to increase education funding, particularly from international corporations who often use the resources and low wages in these nations and pay little in tax (see the Case Study in Chapter 6). In order for this to be effective, UNESCO states that any additional income must target education for the most marginalised children within these nations, the rural populations and girls. Higher income nations have also reduced their aid expenditure to these nations, resulting in less aid focusing on education. For UNESCO the challenges in achieving global education targets mean ensuring governments of high income nations honour their commitments to donate aid, and governments of low and middle income nations increase spending on education. The aims of the founders of UNESCO are certainly worthy, but the translation of those aims into workable, practical actions is extremely difficult. It is clear, however, that low, middle and high income nations all use the education of children and young people as a response to external economic pressures.

The Organisation for Economic Cooperation and Development (OECD)

Many of the recent changes that individual nations have made to their education systems show marked similarities. Just as UNESCO urges low income nations to adopt policies to meet international educational goals, so higher income nations also respond to international organisations; one of the most influential of these is the OECD. The OECD has 31 member states and its engagement in education is primarily through its Programme of International Student Assessment (PISA).

The OECD uses PISA to make international comparisons of education systems. In 2012, 15-year-olds from 65 nations took a set of standardised assessment tests in reading, mathematics and science (see Further Reading for the 2012 results and for examples of the assessment questions).

Since 2000 the OECD has used the results of these quantifiable assessments to make recommendations about education policies based on their findings of best practice. In doing so the OECD is creating one of the most powerful international models for education. The idea of human capital to which Bell and Stevenson (2006) refer has resulted in nations using international recommendations such as those from the OECD to improve children's performance in assessment systems such as PISA. Bieber and Martens argue that this has resulted in the OECD demonstrating *soft governance* (Bieber and Martens, 2011, p 111), which results in a greater convergence of education systems. Individual nations use the experiences of other nations, share problem-solving with other similar nations and copy the education policies from nations seen to be successful in a particular area. In this way the education systems of nations increasingly converge in order to demonstrate better performance in league tables such as PISA and in the belief that this will develop a workforce better able to compete in a global economy. The results of the PISA scores are frequently presented to the public either by politicians who use them to justify education policy decisions in order to improve a nation's ranking or by teachers to demonstrate a need for greater funding or by the media to praise a country's ranking or to criticise. However, even for those nations that do take note of the PISA ranking (Bieber and Martens (2011) note the lack of interest the United States has in the PISA scores), what is clear is the way it generates a public debate about the role of education with rarely any analysis of the actual tests (Pons, 2011). The debate is often limited to discussions of rankings and less upon the focus the OECD places on ensuring social and gender equity in education to support economic well-being. What the OECD demonstrates is the current high level of emphasis placed upon the testing and benchmarking of children's education on both a national and international level.

The Council of Europe (CoE)

UNESCO and the OECD are examples of international organisations with a global reach which have a substantial membership. For UNESCO this arguably results in problems with reaching consensus for ensuring rights to education, and for the OECD this has resulted in creating competition in education between nations. The CoE in comparison is a more regional organisation comprising 47 member nations from across Europe, 28 of which are also members of the European Union. Started in 1946, it has a rights-based approach, with all member states signed up to the European Convention on Human Rights. It aims to promote cultural identity and awareness, find common solutions to challenges facing European societies and support democratic stability in Europe. In terms of education, the CoE seeks to address education disparities across Europe through international co-operation and sharing of information and teaching resources. The Pestalozzi Programme offers educators across Europe access to training and capacity building resources and collaborative projects. This supports a focus on education as a means of promoting citizenship and human rights in line with the aims of the CoE rather than as a means of promoting economic well-being and competition.

As with PISA the CoE also represents a converging of education programmes and international co-operation; however, this is achieved through a drive for collaborative projects. The outcome of convergence through the CoE is one of mutual benefit to all collaborating nations in order to increase social and cultural co-operation rather than seeking to achieve success for individual nations as PISA does. As it is a regional organisation it is able to focus on issues that are most relevant to Europe rather than the broader remits of the other two organisations. An example of this is the work the CoE does on promoting the recognition of Roma and traveller communities across Europe and providing educators with resources for working with Roma children and teaching about Roma history and culture.

CASE STUDY

Taken from: UNESCO/Council of Europe Expert Meeting. Towards Quality Education for Roma Children: Transition from Early Childhood to Primary Education. September 2007.

The report demonstrates the role of two international organisations in converging education policies, in this case across Europe. It noted that Roma children made up one of the most marginalised groups across Europe, and hence the need for a strategy of proactive policies across member nations. The report identified that member states of the CoE in Central and Eastern Europe have prepared and adopted national strategies to support Roma communities. However, it also stated that 50 per cent of Roma children in Europe failed to complete primary education, and in some Eastern European nations between 50 and 80 per cent of Roma children enrolled in schools were transferred to *special schools* originally established for children with learning disabilities. The enrolment rates of Roma children into preschool provision was even lower, with 16–17 per cent enrolled in preschool education in Bulgaria and Romania compared with a national average of 75 per cent. The report identified that improving access to early childhood education settings for Roma and other marginalised children required addressing issues of prejudice and discrimination both within and outside settings and that providing both Roma and non-Roma children with opportunities to learn about and appreciate different cultures including Roma culture would support inclusive learning.

Critical questions

Use the case study above to reflect upon the role international organisations have in shaping national education policies.

» *In your opinion, what significance does the creation of international goals on education have for contemporary childhood experiences? Justify your answer.*

» Examine the current UK education policy to analyse how these international organisations have influenced its creation?

» If education policy in the United Kingdom is influenced by these organisations, how might parents and teachers influence education?

» How effective are the local policies in your area for integrating gypsy, Roma and traveller children into education?

How international organisations shape national policies on education

The first part of this chapter demonstrated how international organisations are creating a convergent approach to education within individual nations. This part now examines what this means on the meso level as it looks at individual nations' education policies and curricula to consider how they are influenced by internal politics and social changes and how international approaches to education have influenced them.

The first example examines the case of the Polish education system. It reviews how the social and political change from communism to democracy has impacted upon the approach successive governments have taken to children's education.

The second example to be considered is how international organisations and studies are shaping the professionalising of the early childhood education and care sector and the dilemmas that emerge about what a professional workforce should look like.

Changes to Poland's education system

Poland, like many Central and Eastern European nations, has undergone significant changes in its political and social structures in the past 25 years. In 1989 Poland moved from a communist to a democratic nation, and fundamental changes were made to its social structures including its education system to meet these new political, social and economic changes. The old communist education system was initially reformed to better fit a democratic nation. Communist ideology and biased views of history were removed from the curriculum, the compulsory requirement to learn Russian was halted and other foreign languages were introduced with opportunities made available for the opening of private education facilities.

The Polish government based the new education system around the United Nations Universal Declaration of Human Rights (UDHR) and the United Nations Convention on the Rights of the Child (UNCRC). It was based upon teaching children to value democracy, tolerance and individual rights and to respect the law. However, problems in the economy saw cuts to education which were frequently seen as a way of saving money on an expensive system. This led successive governments to focus on the number of teaching hours, combining classes and reducing group activities; while this favoured a didactic teaching approach which traditional training had prepared teachers for (Pecherski, 1975) it also meant that meaningful reform to the education system was slow. This continued throughout the 1990s, with the only area of growth in education being the newly created private education institutes which, with good facilities and well trained staff, became popular among the growing middle classes. The state run education system was based heavily on a strict didactic and authoritarian approach to education which arguably did not enable students to develop wider competencies in applying skills and questioning knowledge. Tomiak (2000) notes that several reports conducted by the OECD during the 1990s made recommendations about urgent reform to the education system; however, these were not responded to until 1999.

In 1999, following consultations with public bodies, teachers, parents and the Church as well as the OECD, reforms were implemented to the structure and the curriculum for children in Polish schools. Compulsory schooling begins at 7 years of age and extends till 18 years of age. Polish children start with a primary school cycle of 6 years with a standardised test at the end, followed by a lower secondary school cycle of 3 years. At 16 years, students choose between higher secondary school tracks of either 3 years in general high school, 3 years basic vocational studies or 4 years technical high school. Schools have autonomy in the curriculum built around a core (World Bank, 2010) as well as in the introduction of teaching students key competencies in successful communication, teamwork, problem-solving and computer and internet technology (Dąbrowski and Wiśniewski, 2011). However, Dąbrowski and Wiśniewski (2011) maintain that the Western-based idea of key competencies, as they are not assessed, are not adhered to and traditional teaching methods, used before the education reform, remain favoured in the education system. Further changes were made to the core curriculum in 2002, 2009 and 2012 (Śkliwowski and Grodecka, 2013). Poland now shows marked improvements in its performance in the PISA tests, ranking 14th in 2012 (OECD, 2014).

Critical questions

Compare the Polish model of education to that in the United Kingdom.

» *What evidence of convergence through engagement with international organisations can you see in both models?*

» *Which features could be considered unique to Poland or the United Kingdom?*

» *In your opinion, how has the view of education as a means to achieve economic well-being influenced decision-making in Poland?*

» *To extend this analysis, examine research conducted into the experiences of Polish children attending British schools.*

Professionalising staff in early childhood education and care

Early childhood education and care (ECEC) is a part of the education sector experiencing some of the most rapid changes from both international and national perspectives. The emerging evidence of the social and economic benefits of high quality early years provision, particularly for managing social inequality and later educational attainment of socio-economically disadvantaged children, has brought attention to the professional qualifications and status of practitioners working in the sector in order to meet these needs (Oberhuemer, 2011). A number of international studies have drawn conclusions on best practice, which has sparked a debate within high and higher income nations on the professional identity of practitioners who work with children from 3 to 6 years of age and for those who work with children under 3 years.

In 2001 the OECD published *Starting Strong* (OECD, 2001) – the results of a project which reviewed the ECEC in 20 nations and drew a number of conclusions on best practice. It identified eight key elements of best practice in promoting quality ECEC and advised that they be adopted by nations in order to meet a range of challenges, from reducing child poverty to promoting gender equality and diversity. One of the factors of the advised approach was to ensure appropriate training and working conditions for the staff. In 2006 *Starting Strong II* (OECD, 2006) was published. It was an analysis of the developments, issues and further policy options derived from examining the progress the 20 nations had made, and it concluded with ten recommendations for future ECEC policies. One of its recommendations again emphasised the importance of improving the working conditions and professional qualifications of the ECEC staff. In 2011 the Council of the European Union (Council of the European Union, 2011) agreed eight measures for member states to support ECEC within their nations, from improving access to high quality ECEC, particularly for children from socioeconomic disadvantage, migrant or Roma backgrounds or children with special educational needs (SEN). The report also recommended supporting the professionalising of ECEC staff, developing competencies and qualifications and working conditions in order to enhance the prestige of the profession and to attract and retain suitably qualified staff and improve the workforce gender imbalance.

As Oberhuemer (2011) observed, what has now emerged is a divergent understanding and approach by many of these nations to the requirements for professional staff working with children under 6 years of age and how to implement a professional workforce. However, what is meant by a professional workforce and what they are expected to value has become an area of much contention. The role of ECEC as a means of addressing social and economic disadvantages has led a number of nations to promote the education of young children over their care (Moss and Cameron, 2011). This has meant that for some nations professionalising the ECEC workforce has resulted in dividing the education from the care role of ECEC staff, focusing on the delivery of education targets as part of a professional role with the notion of care being the role of assistants who are less qualified and receive lower pay (Van Laere et al, 2012). While reports such as those by the OECD were not intended to favour *education* over *care,* what has emerged is that the approach to professionalising ECEC staff in a number of nations, particularly across Europe, has made this division, rather than taking a more holistic approach to working with children under six years of age. What this demonstrates is that one of the drawbacks of creating international recommendations is the way these are translated into policy on a national level.

Critical questions

Reflect upon the section above and the idea of professionalising the ECEC workforce.

» *How does the professionalising of the ECEC workforce relate to a view of young children as a productive investment by international organisations and national governments?*

» *The section highlights that policies push those working with young children to prioritise education over care. How might this division of education and care impact not only upon young children but also older children throughout their education?*

» *How could the separation of education and care have a positive impact?*

» *How might prioritising education over care influence the way practitioners interact with parents and carers? Justify your argument.*

Limitations with developing convergent education systems

Having analysed how international organisations and nations develop convergent education systems, this final section evaluates some limitations and problems with developing these convergent models of education.

Firstly, it considers the introduction of standardised testing as part of the current developments in education both internationally and nationally. The limitations of this model are analysed by reflecting on how this works in China and Norway.

Secondly, a cultural aspect of educational systems, classroom discipline, is examined. The diverse cultural expectations regarding children's education is reflected in the approaches taken to classroom discipline. The meaning of discipline and the way it is managed is explored through analysing international studies in line with children's rights and national legislation.

The use of standardised testing as an education model

The push to develop education policies with clearly defined standards has become an aspect common to convergent global education. As McNeil (2000) argues, these standards can take the form of either broad goals, such as those identified in the Starting Strong projects (OECD, 2001; 2006) discussed earlier, or increasingly narrowly defined targets as measured through standardised testing. Accountability in teaching and learning is an important factor in these convergent global education systems, standardised testing through both formative and summative assessments being the means by which these are frequently measured.

There has always been a need to balance equity with rigour in the use of standardised testing for the assessment of learning in order to demonstrate fairness. However, the increasing importance placed on the outcomes of standardised tests means reliability has become a driving force. This has arguably led to prioritising factual knowledge which can be measured above other learning skills such as attitudes. In the United Kingdom, in 1991, national curriculum assessments (commonly referred to as Standardised Assessment Tasks or SATs) were introduced into the curriculum in all maintained primary and secondary schools to test English, mathematics and science. The SATs require the standardised testing of seven-year-olds at the end of Key Stage 1 (KS1) and 11-year-olds at the end of Key Stage 2 (KS2), and results have been measured through eight-level descriptors of increasing difficulty. From September 2015 the levels will be replaced by a relative measure, so children will receive a score scaled out of 100, making comparison possible between a child's score at the end of KS1 with their score at the end of KS2. (See Further Reading for more information on national curricula reform and SATs.)

Standardised tests, whether in an international form such as the PISA tests (OECD, 2014) or in the form of national tests such as SATs, used increasingly within nations to measure attainment at key stages in a child's education, face two significant challenges.

1. Does standardised testing improve the education of all children, particularly the least advantaged?

2. Does standardised testing improve the quality of the curriculum and teaching?

Does standardised testing improve the education of all children?

Standardised testing reflects a neoliberal, centralised approach to education, heavily influenced by a business model mentality, which deliberately ignores social, racial and linguistic difference and instead upholds a power-based, procrustean approach to education that favours the cultural and linguistic model represented within the test. Education becomes a system of technical skills which do not necessarily reflect the social and cultural experience of the communities that the least advantaged children recognise or respond to. The focus is placed upon the education system rather than on children's experience of schooling. The importance of engaging in tangible learning relevant to children's experiences is replaced by an abstract approach influenced by the need to attain test scores. This is particularly the case for children from communities whose experiences are not reflected in the culture of the standardised test.

The result is that standardised testing risks creating a *well-educated* student based more upon their ability to succeed at a test rather than their ability demonstrated through a broader assessment of knowledge. Özturgut (2011), reviewing the impact of a long history of standardised testing in the Chinese education system, maintains that this has led to elitism among the student population. The demand for supplementary support programmes to prepare for tests means only those parents best able to afford the cost of tutoring can send their children to elite schools. Those children whose parents can either not afford the tutoring or who have not had access to additional support programmes quickly become marginalised within such an education system. While standardised tests focus on a narrow concept of learning which risks marginalising children with fewer advantages, they do present a nation's policy-makers with quantitative data which are typically used to measure quality and *standards* in education. If these cannot be proven then the value of standardised testing might be called into question. This leads to the second point.

Does standardised testing improve the quality of both the curriculum and teaching?

The OECD highlights the importance of inclusive and equitable education systems as necessary for ensuring good quality (OECD, 2006). Standardised testing as a means of determining accountability for the quality of teaching and learning has become the benchmark for measuring excellence and consequently impacted the curriculum and teaching in two important ways.

- Rather than being the measure of successful understanding of the curriculum, standardised testing has become a more integral part of shaping the curriculum. The limitations of what can be assessed in this type of testing has led to higher value being placed upon areas of the curriculum best suited to this style. So the focus on core curriculum around literacy, numeracy and science has marginalised more creative subjects with their inherent skills of problem solving, creative thinking and expression and reasoning. As Őzturgut (2011) observes, standardised testing creates uniformity and conformity to the curriculum.

- While standardised tests offer a means by which a student and a teacher might be able to assess progress within specific areas of learning, the requirement that the tests be made public and become part of local, national or international league tables presents particular dilemmas. Mausethagen's (2013) study of teachers' reactions to the standardised testing in Norway reports how they struggle to understand the role of testing as a fair measure of the quality of their teaching and begin to legitimise supporting children to practise and prepare for the tests they will be taking. The use of standardised testing risks the often formatted critique that teachers will *teach to the test* or at least engage children in practising for tests, whether that is justified as a means of protecting and preparing them, meeting parental concerns or to ensure that a school performs well in a league table of published results. It is also important to consider how standardised testing might influence the approaches to discipline taken within classrooms.

The way the public and parents respond to the publication of the results of standardised national tests is significant in their role as accountability tools. However, in these discussions the role of children is rarely examined. In the following case study the positioning of children in the media and discussion of national testing results in Australia is examined.

CASE STUDY

Lange, T and Meaney, T (2014) It's Just As Well Kids Don't Vote: The Positioning of Children Through Public Discourse Around National Testing. Mathematics Education Research Journal. *26: pp 377–397.*

This study examines how children are positioned in discussions the Australian public and politicians engage in following the publication of national testing results. Achieving minimum standards in mathematics and literacy are widely regarded as essential to obtaining a *good* education. The researchers used interview transcripts, media releases and online news reports with public comments to examine how children were positioned in the discussion of national testing. Five themes emerged.

1. *Educational responsibilities for children*. The support that was offered to children was discussed, the balance of responsibilities between teachers and parents was hotly debated. Within this discussion the researchers report that children were positioned as objects for support, with little control.

2.   *Children as objects*. The researchers found that children tended to be seen as objects whose values could be measured. It was noted that politicians tended to refer to parents as *consumers* with the testing of children needed in order that the results could be documented and reported to parents. Parents who engaged in discussion reported a wish to be informed in order to make choices about their children's education and the value that could be added to their education.

3.   *Children constructed as disadvantaged*. While the researchers argued that children were positioned as commodities it was also recognised that not all children could be expected to gain the same value. The positioning of children as disadvantaged was connected to schools that were also being labelled as disadvantaged. The discussions identified disadvantaged children as indigenous children, children with disability, children from poorer households and gifted children. These children were positioned as least likely to gain added value to their education. Some parents felt that the labelling of a school as disadvantaged impacted their children's life chances as a consequence of attending that school. To these children national testing was not a neutral or benign tool.

4.   *Purpose of education*. The government website presented information about test results as purely objective and neutral and therefore incontestable. The researchers argue this resulted in little public discussion regarding what education is and what schools should be, beyond a *good education*. The value added to children arguably held greater importance than the kind of education that generated that value. The discussion on the results for mathematics identified gaining a *good* mathematical education as important without clarifying why, beyond employment or university entrance.

5.   *Children's agency and learning*. The researchers noted that beyond the main positioning of children as commodities there was evidence of children being discussed with regard to their own agency, mainly in terms of their interaction with teachers without specifying what that meant. Generally, however, children were not seen as active agents in their learning.

The researchers concluded that the public discussion of test results tended to show children as commodities that could have value added to them through education. The individual needs of children and their agency was not a major consideration. The idea of parental choice for parents as a result of publishing test results was contested as low income families felt they did not have the same choices available to them as wealthier families. The creation of disadvantage as a result of the publication of test results was responded to through raising school accountability rather than ideas of social justice. The value and validity of what was being measured was not considered, except for the amount of data. The result was a focus on minimum standards that the researchers identified limited the education of children.

As the case study identifies, national standardised testing has become a feature of convergent education models. The role standardised tests play in the education policies of governments mean they have become powerful policy levers. There is a need, however, to examine what such tests are able to measure and acknowledge what they cannot.

Critical questions

Standardised testing has become an integral part of the educational experiences of children across a growing number of nations.

» *What benefits can be gained from integrating standardised testing into national education policies?*

» *In your opinion, what achievements cannot be measured through standardised testing of children? Justify your explanation and consider how these achievements could be measured.*

» *Critically reflect upon the case study to analyse how the public debate of national standardised test results could be broadened?*

» *In your opinion, what could be done to maximise children's agency in the debate on standardised attainment testing? Justify your answer with reference to current systems.*

Classroom discipline

The UNCRC (UN, 1989) advocates the protection of a set of non-negotiable children's rights necessary to meet their basic needs (see Chapter 5). Their basis in the fundamental right to dignity regardless of gender, race, religion or culture has been used in the formulation of legislation concerning children within ratifying nations. Under Article 28 (2) – the Right to Education – the Convention states *'Parties shall take all appropriate measures to ensure that school discipline is administered in a manner consistent with the child's human dignity and in conformity with the present Convention'*. The UNCRC recognises the importance of classroom discipline to promote children's learning through facilitating an equitable learning environment and responsibility through internalising self-control and self-discipline (Chiu and Chow, 2011). However, in the light of ever-converging systems of education, the pressure to demonstrate success in standardised tests and a universal rights-based approach to the care and protection of children, the approach to discipline within different nations is an area of growing research interest. The challenge to the study of classroom discipline is the premise of what constitutes discipline in terms of the UNCRC.

In a highly quantitative study using the results from OECD PISA 2002 questionnaires, Chiu and Chow (2011) explored classroom discipline in terms of how a nation's economy, culture and schools influence children's reports of classroom discipline. Examining 41 nations, Chiu and Chow concluded that poorer, more equal or, conversely, less gender egalitarian nations demonstrated higher classroom discipline than richer nations. However, PISA (OECD, 2011) reported a rise in school discipline and improved teacher–student relationships across most nations, including wealthier nations between 2000 and 2009. Yet neither of these studies examine what constitutes good discipline and what this means in terms of the UNCRC's premise that it be '*administered in a manner consistent with the child's human dignity*' (UN, 1989). While all the nations in the PISA studies ratified the UNCRC (with the exception of the United States) it is worth exploring what this means by considering some qualitative studies.

While the use of corporal punishment as a form of classroom discipline may be legislated against in many nations, this does not necessarily guarantee that it is not practised. Rajdev (2012) highlights that in India and China, despite being legislated against, corporal punishment continues, particularly in rural areas. In the US corporal punishment is permitted in a number of states with physical punishments being administered to black boys more frequently than any other group of children (Rajdev, 2012).

As part of the converging of education systems, effective classroom discipline techniques across nations have become an area of much discussion. Classroom discipline, in terms more closely associated with the UNCRC, now generally focuses on three broad approaches:

1.   the application of rewards and punishments by teachers against a set of clearly defined behaviour expectations;

2.   children's self-regulation of behaviour through negotiation and the implementation of behaviour contracts with teachers;

3.   group participation and decision-making with children taking responsibility for their class behaviour.

Lewis et al (2008) note how in practice most behaviour strategies combine elements of all three approaches. In a study of classroom discipline techniques across Israel, Australia and China, behaviour management techniques that involved increasing the severity of punishments when they are resisted or anger, shouting at or humiliating children were associated with poor classroom discipline and negative attitudes towards learning by children (Lewis et al, 2008). They found that recognising and reinforcing positive behaviour, particularly for children who doubt their competence in this, and discussing the impact of their behaviour on others were the most effective strategies; hinting at unacceptable behaviour without punishment and negotiating behaviour expectations with children were seen as moderately effective. While these techniques impacted positively on the children's approach to learning, aggression and increasing severity of punishments were the least effective and could generate negative approaches by children to their learning.

Lewis (2001) reports that an Australian study on children's views of the impact of different behaviour strategies found that boys were more likely to misbehave and act irresponsibly than girls, and children who are more interested in their school work and think it important are more likely to act responsibly. Lewis (2001) suggests that as children transfer from primary to secondary education, a combination of hormonal changes, sub-group cultures that favour not acting responsibly, and reduced recognition and empowerment within secondary school influence their behaviour.

Critical questions

» How would you analyse the effectiveness of the behaviour strategies identified above? Use research evidence into these strategies to justify your conclusions.

» How would you evaluate the effectiveness of the behaviour strategies within your setting? Create a plan for how this would be achieved.

» How would you make a distinction between the benefits and limitations of using different behaviour strategies among different groups of children in a setting?

» How might the view of education as something intrinsically valuable in its own right influence the approaches taken to classroom discipline? Justify your conclusion with reference to your own research.

Critical reflections

This chapter has examined the role international organisations play in the educational experiences of children globally. It started by considering Bell and Stevenson's (2006) premise that education has become a commodity used to ensure economic well-being rather than something intrinsically valuable in its own right. You should review the answers you gave to the critical questions at the start of this chapter and reflect on whether your ideas have changed or developed as a result of the issues explored.

It is important that those working in the education and care of children recognise the influences that shape national policies towards a convergent education system and are able to reflect upon what the implications of this might be, not only for professional identity but also for the children and families in your care. The value and limitations of examining aspects of education from an international perspective are likely to become increasingly important as the pressures continue on those working with children and young people to prepare them for becoming part of a nation's economic well-being.

Further reading

Council of Europe: Education. Includes links to the Pestalozzi Programme of resources and projects. Available at: www.coe.int/t/dg4/education/

Education for All (EfA). An expanded vision of inclusive learning. Available at: www.unesco.org.uk/education_for_all

Education for All (EfA) Global Monitoring Report 2013/14. Available at: www.efareport.unesco.org

Hageman, K, Jarausch, K and Allemann-Ghionda, C (eds) (2014) *Children, Families and States: Time Policies of Childcare, Preschool, and Primary Education in Europe.* Oxford: Berghahn.

Information on PISA. Available at: www.oecd.org/pisa/

SATs and national curriculum reform in the United Kingdom. Information available at: https://www.gov.uk/government/organisations/standards-and-testing-agency

References

Bell, L and Stevenson, H (2006) *Education Policy: Process, Themes and Impact*. London: Routledge.

Bieber, T and Martens, K (2011) The OECD PISA Study as a Soft Power in Education? Lessons from Switzerland and the US. *European Journal of Education*. 46 (1): pp 101–116.

Chiu, M and Chow, B (2011) Classroom Discipline across Forty-One Countries: School, Economic and Cultural Differences. *Journal of Cross-Cultural Psychology*. 42 (3): pp 516–533.

Council of the European Union (2011) *Council Conclusions on Early Childhood Education and Acre: Providing All Our Children with the Best Start for the World of Tomorrow*. Brussels: Council of the European Union.

Dąbrowski, M and Wiśniewski, J (2011) Translating Key Competences into the School Curriculum: Lessons from the Polish Experience. *European Journal of Education*. 46 (3): pp 323–334.

Lange, T and Meaney, T (2014) It's Just as Well Kids Don't Vote: The Positioning of Children through Public Discourse around National Testing. *Mathematics Education Research Journal*. 26: pp 377–397.

Lewis, R (2001) Classroom Discipline and Student Responsibility: The Students' View. *Teaching and Teacher Education*. 17: pp 307–319.

Lewis, R, Romi, S, Katz, Y and Qui, X (2008) Students' Reaction to Classroom Discipline in Australia, Israel, and China. *Teaching and Teacher Education*. 24: pp 715–724.

Mausethagen, S (2013) Talking About the Test. Boundary Work in Primary School Teachers' Interactions Around National Testing of Student Performance. *Teaching and Teacher Education*. 36: pp 132–142.

McNeil, L (2000) *Educational Costs of Standardized Testing*. London: Routledge.

Moss, P and Cameron, C (2011) Social Pedagogy: Future Directions?, in Cameron, C and Moss, P (eds) *Social Pedagogy and Working with Children and Young People. Where Care and Education Meet*. London: Jessica Kingsley Publishers.

Oberhuemer, P (2011) The Early Childhood Education Workforce in Europe Between Divergencies and Emergencies. *International Journal of Child Care and Education Policy*. 5 (1): pp 55–63.

OECD (2001) *Starting Strong: Early Childhood Education and Care*. Paris: OECD Education and Training Division.

OECD (2006) *Starting Strong II: Early Childhood Education and Care*. Paris: OECD Education and Training Division.

OECD (2011) PISA in Focus 4: Has Discipline in Schools Deteriorated? [online] Available at: www.pisa.oecd.org (accessed 22 July 2014).

OECD (2014) PISA 2012 Results in Focus: What 15-Year-Olds Know and What They Can Do with What They Know. [online] Available at: www.oecd.org/pisa/keyfindings/pisa-2012-results-overview.pdf (accessed 17 July 2014).

Özturgut, O (2011) Standardized Testing in the Case of China and the Lessons to Be Learned for the U.S. *Journal of International Education Research*. 7 (2): pp 1–6.

Pecherski, M (1975) Changes in the Polish System of Education since 1972. *International Review of Education*. 21 (4): pp 407–421.

Pons, X (2011) What Do We Really Learn from PISA? The Sociology of Its Reception in Three European Countries (201–2008) *European Journal of Education*. 46 (4): pp 540–548.

Rajdev, U (2012) Ethics and Corporal Punishment within the Schools Across the Globe. *Journal of International Education Research*. 8 (2): pp 165–172.

Śkliwowski, K and Grodecka, K (2013) *Open Educational Resources in Poland: Challenges and Opportunities*. Moscow: UNESCO.

Tomiak, J (2000) Polish Education Facing the Twenty-first Century: Dilemmas and Difficulties. *Comparative Education*. 36 (2): pp 177–186.

UN (2014) Millennium Development Goals and Beyond 2015. [online] Available at: www.un.org/millenniumgoals/ (accessed 15 July 2014).

UNESCO (1945) Constitution of the United Nations Educational, Scientific and Cultural Organization (UNESCO). [online] Available at: http://portal.unesco.org/en/ev.php-URL_ID=15244andURL_DO=DO_TOPICandURL_SECTION=201.html (accessed 15 July 2014).

UNESCO/Council of Europe Expert Meeting (2007) *Towards Quality Education for Roma Children: Transition from Early Childhood to Primary Education*. UNESCO.

UNESCO (2014) EfA Global Monitoring Report 2013/14. Teaching and Learning: Achieving Quality for All. [online] Available at: www.efareport.unesco.org (accessed 15 July 2014).

Van Laere, K, Peeters, J and Vandenbroeck, M (2012) The Education and Care Divide: The Role of the Early Childhood Workforce in 15 European Countries. *European Journal of Education*. 47 (4): pp 527–541.

World Bank (2010) Europe and Central Asia Knowledge Brief: Successful Education Reform: Lessons from Poland. [online] Available at: http://web.worldbank.org/WBSITE/EXTERNAL/COUNTRIES/ECAEXT/0,,contentMDK:22767787~pagePK:146736~piPK:146830~theSitePK:258599,00.html (accessed 18 July 2014).

5 Children's rights and children's needs

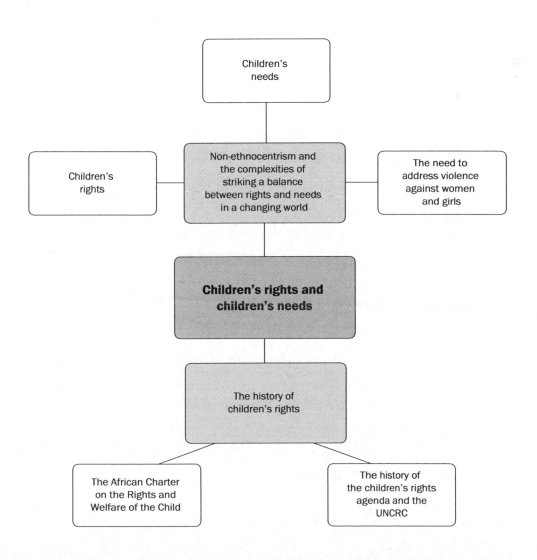

Children's
needs

Children's
rights

Non-ethnocentrism and
the complexities of
striking a balance
between rights and needs
in a changing world

The need to
address violence
against women
and girls

**Children's rights and
children's needs**

The history of
children's rights

The African Charter
on the Rights and
Welfare of the Child

The history of
the children's rights
agenda and the
UNCRC

The child, by reason of his physical and mental immaturity, needs special safeguards and care, including appropriate legal protection, before as well as after birth.
(Declaration of the Rights of the Child, UN, 1959)

Introduction

The quote above demonstrates the prevailing view, taken in 1959, of children's physical and mental immaturity defining childhood. While this view might be challenged in the contemporary view of children, the idea that *the child 'needs special safeguards and care'* remains. This chapter examines the complex relationship between two fundamental aspects to the study of contemporary childhoods – the children's rights agenda and the concept of children's needs. These two areas are brought together in this chapter to develop a critical analysis of how they both impact upon children's lives. The way in which children's needs are identified, measured and met and the role of the children's rights agenda is analysed with regard to ethnocentrism and the challenge of taking a non-ethnocentric approach to the topic (see Chapter 1 for a full discussion of non-ethnocentrism). This chapter is divided into two parts:

1. the history of children's rights;

2. non-ethnocentrism and the complexities of striking a balance between rights and needs in a changing world.

The chapter begins with a historical overview of the children's rights agenda and its relationship with the changing understanding of what it is that children need and how this led to the development of the United Nations Convention on the Rights of the Child (UNCRC) and the African Charter on the Rights and Welfare of the Child (ACRWC). The chapter continues to examine the influence that such definitions of *rights* and *needs* have upon contemporary childhoods and the challenges of non-ethnocentrism when they are viewed from an international perspective. Challenges such as violence against women and girls (VAWG), children's needs and child labour are analysed in terms of the complexities of the socio-cultural and power elements that impact upon addressing children's needs and the children's rights agenda.

Critical questions

» *How are the features of children's physical and mental immaturity likely to influence the approach taken to children's rights and needs?*

» *How would you classify needs for safeguarding and care that are special to children?*

» *In your opinion, which of these needs could be considered as universal and which as culturally or socially specific? Justify your argument.*

» *If some needs might be considered socially or culturally specific what are the challenges facing a universal rights agenda to ensure all children's needs are met?*

The history of children's rights

Defining the terms used in the discussion of any issue not only helps clarify common starting points but also helps identify the complexities and limitations. Children's rights are generally understood to be composed of three broad strands – provision, protection and participation.

- Provision rights – seek to ensure the resources and skills are in place for children to survive, thrive and develop and to ensure the other two rights strands are met.

- Protection rights – seek to protect children from harm, abuse or exploitation by individuals, organisations or governments. These include physical, emotional and psychological harm as well as the protection of the rights to access the other two strands.

- Participation rights – seek to ensure children can participate in processes that involve the other strands of their rights and are active agents in decisions that affect their lives on an individual and wider social level.

The interactions between these strands can be supportive and mutually beneficial, for example the provision of free primary education supports children's protection and participation. Conversely, these strands can also be contradictory and at times mutually incompatible and these present some of the major challenges to enacting children's rights internationally. For example, later in this chapter, the challenges around child labour are considered. The concept of rights, whether adult or child, contains the obligation that an action must be taken to ensure that right; how that action is managed and decisions regarding who has the responsibility for completing it raises a number of questions which will be discussed in part two of this chapter.

Similarly children's *needs* present a complex concept. The notion of children having needs has evolved in the context of the changing ideas about what childhood is (see Chapter 2) and has become an integral part of the modern view of childhood. Indeed it has become so entrenched in the twentieth and twenty-first century perspective of childhood that what it means is rarely held up for scrutiny. In a detailed analysis of how children's needs have become part of the lexicon of childhood studies, Martin Woodhead (Woodhead, 1997) argues that children's needs suggest a universal element to childhood which can be highly emotive. Through the language of needs an underlying element of power is created. Just as the child's rights require an obligation to action, similarly in order for needs to be met, Woodhead (1997) proposes, an action must be taken. In taking that action control is generated that positions the subject of the action (the child) as dependent upon the person carrying out the action (generally an adult). What this means in relation to the children's rights agenda is analysed in depth later in the chapter; however, first it is useful to consider the history of the children's rights agenda.

The history of the children's rights agenda and the UNCRC

Children's rights and children's needs are rooted in Western historical movements for political, economic and social reform. The international movement for children's rights initially focused on children's need for protection and began as part of the broader push for welfare reform in Europe dating back to the mid-nineteenth century. This aimed to move away from the punishment of children and towards addressing the social conditions that would prevent child neglect and delinquency (Fuchs, 2008). The outbreak of the First World War meant an international agreement was stalled until the postwar foundation of the League of Nations in

1919 which established the Committee for the Protection of Children. The establishment of a Bureau for Child Welfare saw international co-operation continue to focus on child protection. It was decided that education should remain within national control, and instead the League concentrated on researching issues such as crime, child protection and child labour (Fuchs, 2008). In 1924 the Declaration of the Rights of the Child saw the start of the international children's rights agenda which codified a set of rights based on child welfare (Wyness, 2006) and which a year later also saw the introduction of education into the agenda.

It was not until after the Second World War in 1946 that the United Nations Children's Fund (UNICEF) was founded and took over the role of the Bureau for Child Welfare. In 1948 the Declaration on Human Rights and the eventual Declaration of the Rights of the Child in 1959 defined the duties and responsibilities of the state and of parents, which led to greater involvement of non-governmental organisations (NGOs), such as Save the Children and the Catholic Agency for Overseas Development (CAFOD), in supporting children's rights to development, protection and free education and also in identifying children's social and cultural rights. This resulted in children's rights being tied to a nation's economic development (see Chapter 6).

The twentieth anniversary of the Declaration of the Rights of the Child in 1979 was named the International Year of the Child. This helped renew attention on children's needs and on the process of drawing up a new children's rights convention, and, unlike in 1959, input from NGOs as well as individual national governments was included. In 1989 the United Nations Convention on the Rights of the Child (UNCRC) (UN, 1989) was ratified by the General Assembly and the UN Committee on the Rights of the Child (CRC), enshrined in the UNCRC. Composed of 18 independent experts, the CRC was formed to monitor the implementation of the UNCRC by the signatory nations. Each signatory nation must submit a report to the CRC two years after becoming a signatory to the Convention and then must submit the report every five years. (See Further Reading on the work of the CRC.) UNICEF collates children's rights under the Convention into four categories (see Table 5.1).

A fundamental shift brought to the children's rights agenda by the UNCRC was the fourth participatory strand which saw children being given rights to self-determination, and it placed a child's right to education as a fundamental element of the agenda (see Chapter 4 for a discussion on education rights, UNESCO and Education for All).

The principle of participation rights is tempered somewhat by the addition of *evolving capacities* to the text of the Convention. It is the adults who will make a judgement as to the limits of a child's capacity and access to the right, for example, to freedom of thought, expression and religion (Article 14).

An examination of the articles listed above reveals that the rights can generally be divided into positive and negative rights, that is those rights which seek a positive action such as the provision of education (Article 28) and those rights which seek to prevent a harmful action such as the right to prevent children from being used in the drugs trade (Article 33). However, as Hall (2005) argues, taken from an international perspective, the provision rights which require positive actions also require a nation to have the government control, wealth, infrastructure and leadership to be capable of providing these actions (Articles 26 and 27).

Table 5.1 Four categories used by the UNICEF to summarise the United Nations Convention on the Rights of the Child

1. Guiding principles:
• Article 1 – defines a child under the Convention
• Article 2 – identifies the non-discrimination of any children
• Article 3 – identifies that all actions should be in the best interests of the child
• Article 6 – the right to life, survival and development
• Article 12 – respect to be taken for the view of the child
2. Survival and development rights
• Article 4 – the protection of children's rights
• Article 5 – rights of parental guidance by families
• Article 6 – the right to life, survival and development
• Articles 7 and 8   the right to registration, a name, nationality and care and the right to an identity
• Articles 9, 10, 14, 18, 20 and 25 - the right to see both parents if they separate (9), the right to move between countries to be reunited with family (10), the child's right to freedom of thought (14), both parents share responsibility for raising the child (18), children who cannot be raised by their parents have a right to special care (20) and children in the care of the local authority have the right to have these arrangements reviewed regularly (25)
• Article 22 – refugee children have the right to special protection
• Articles 23 and 24 – the right to special care for children with a disability (23), the right to good quality health care (24)
• Articles 26 and 27– children who are poor have the right to help from the government (26) and the right to an adequate standard of living with government helping families to meet this (27)
• Articles 28 and 29 – the right to free primary education (28) and the goals of education should develop the child's personality, talents and abilities (29)
• Article 30 – children from minority or indigenous groups have the right to practice their own culture, language and religion
• Article 31 – the right to relax and play
• Article 42 – governments should make the rights known to adults and children

3. Protection rights
• Article 4 – the protection of children's rights
• Articles 11 and 35 – kidnapping and abduction – children protected from being taken out of their country illegally through parental abduction (11) or trafficking, prostitution or pornography (35)
• Article 19 – the right of the child to be protected from hurt or mistreatment physically or mentally
• Articles 20 and 21 – children who cannot be raised by their parents have a right to special care (20) and the child's right to protection if adopted or fostered (21)
• Article 22 – refugee children have the right to special protection
• Article 32 – governments should protect children from work that is dangerous or might harm their health or education
• Articles 33, 34 and 36 – the right to protection from the use of drugs and being used in the drugs trade (33), protection from all forms of sexual exploitation and abuse (34) and from any activity that takes advantage of them or could harm their welfare and development (36)
• Articles 37 and 40 – the child is not to be punished in a cruel or unusual way including if the child breaks the law (37) and children accused of breaking the law are entitled to legal help and fair treatment (40)
• Article 38 – governments must do all they can to protect and care for children affected by war
• Article 39 – children who are the victims of neglect, abuse or exploitation should receive special help physically and psychologically
4. Participation rights
• Article 12 – respect for the views of the child
• Article 13 – children have the right to get and share information as long as the information is not damaging to them or others
• Article 14 – the child's right to freedom of thought, expression and religion
• Article 15 – freedom of association, the right to meet together, join groups and organisations as long as it does not stop other people from enjoying their rights
• Article 16 – the right to privacy and protection from attack on their good name, family and home
• Article 17 – the right to access to information and mass media that is important to their health and well-being

The capacity for welfare provision reflects a highly Westernised approach to children's rights which the review of the history of children's rights earlier illustrated had built up over centuries. For majority world nations, the postcolonial reality of the twentieth and twenty-first centuries makes this kind of provision a considerable challenge (see Chapter 7 for an examination of postcolonial theory).

A further criticism of the UNCRC is the view of childhood and families which favours an ethnocentric, Western *first world* perspective which expects that parents will prioritise education over work and does not recognise the decisions that poor families must make around their children's education and the need for survival. Similarly the rights concerning the child and the family (Articles 18 and 20) arguably position the nuclear family as the norm (Wyness, 2006) which is not the case across much of the world (see Chapter 3 for a discussion of families and parenting). The result of the UNCRC is the inevitable connection between the children's rights agenda and the international development agenda (see Chapter 6) in order to meet the needs of children.

The African Charter on the Rights and Welfare of the Child

In 1999, in response to these challenges, the Organisation of African Unity, which was later replaced by the African Union (AU), adopted the African Charter on the Rights and Welfare of the Child (ACRWC). The ACRWC is the only region-specific rights charter and builds on the UNCRC. It aims to bring a focus on the specific rights and needs of children on the African continent. All member nations of the AU have signed the ACRWC, which like the UNCRC has a committee, the African Committee of Experts on the Rights and Welfare of the Child, to which signatories submit reports two years after signing and then every three years. The ACRWC created rights specifically relevant to Africa such as apartheid, risks specific to girls (such as female genital mutilation (FGM) and early marriage), how a child is defined, children of imprisoned mothers, the African concept of community and the duties and responsibilities of the child towards the family and community. (See Further Reading for information on the ACRWC). However, some aspects of the ACRWC sit in sharp contrast to the UNCRC, such as Article 31 which defines the responsibilities of the child *'to respect his parents, superiors and elders at all times and to assist them in case of need'* (ACRWC, 1990). This reflects a perspective of childhood that challenges the individualistic view of the child reflected in the UNCRC. Unlike the UNCRC the ACRWC does recognise specific protection rights based on gender as demonstrated in Article 21 which states: *'Protection against Harmful Social and Cultural Practices: those customs and practices discriminatory to the child on the grounds of sex or other status'* (ACRWC, 1990). The ACRWC also does not make any allowance for minority groups, unlike the UNCRC, which can be considered an issue as there are a number of ethnic minority groups across Africa.

Critical questions

Reflect upon the development of children's rights.

» *How has the children's rights agenda influenced policy-making in your area of practice?*

» *What impact has the UNCRC had on your practice with children and families?*

» *In your opinion, what are the advantages and disadvantages of Africa having its own children's rights charter?*

Non-ethnocentrism and the complexities of striking a balance between rights and needs in a changing world

Children's needs

As discussed earlier, children's needs require close analysis in order to recognise two important aspects – the socio-cultural element and the power elements – involved in identifying, measuring and addressing children's needs. In analysing these it is possible to recognise how '*assumptions*' and '*judgements*' (Wyness, 1997, p 63) are made about what children need and how and by whom these needs will be met.

Socio-cultural aspect to children's needs

Policies relating to children's needs tend to accord them universal and timeless qualities. While there are certainly universal aspects to children's needs – consider Maslow's hierarchy of needs, for example – nonetheless a socio-cultural element persists within how these needs are identified, measured and met. Returning to Maslow's hierarchy of needs, the basic biological and psychological needs such as food, drink, shelter, warmth and sleep might be universal, yet they are clearly subject to socio-cultural influences regarding how they are identified, measured and met. Maslow's higher order needs such as self-actualisation, identified as realising personal potential, self-fulfilment and personal growth, also have a socio-cultural element. (Chapter 4 discusses the role education has come to play in addressing many of these needs in the contemporary global society.) Both the UNCRC and the ACRWC demonstrate how the children's rights agenda has come to be one of the most influential and powerful means of identifying, measuring and addressing these needs; how this is done through a non-ethnocentric stance that is able to bridge socio-cultural divides is the challenge that faces universal children's rights when translated into socio-cultural realities. (See Further Reading for how the Department for International Development (DFID) is working to address children's needs such as the protection of girls from FGM and child, early and forced early marriage (CEFM) in communities within the United Kingdom and abroad). This raises the second aspect of children's needs – that of power.

Universal aspects to children's needs

The universalisation of children's needs has led to a general acceptance and legitimacy of actions conducted by governments in the name of the needs of children (Bűhler-Niederberger, 2003). This has served to create a power element to policies aimed at addressing children's needs, placing those who develop and influence those policies in positions of power. Bűhler-Niederberger (2003) argues that this is particularly true of the media, political parties and governments. The result of stating that an action is aimed at meeting the needs of children either within nations or internationally creates what Bǔhler-Niederberger (2003, p 95) terms the naturalisation of the *needy child* who, unlike the *useful child* who contributes to the family income, is rendered economically *useless*. To clarify the point, a review of the UNCRC creates a view of a child who needs protection and provision and who is offered participation as agreed by those adults in authority. The child is arguably positioned as *needy*; this child is not to be made *useful* to the family through economic provision but rather to remain economically *useless* as fits the Western view of childhood. So does this matter? Is it not better for the child to be *needy* than to be *useful* and risk exploitation? Yet as the ACRWC establishes, many communities do not recognise the *needy child* model as the definition of childhood, and seeing children as having responsibilities to their family and community sits at odds with the idea of the economically useless child.

However, Bǔhler-Niederberger's (2003) points out that the 'needy child' has become a naturalised aspect of childhood in the West and therefore 'useful' to policy-makers; this means that it is difficult to argue against policies, charters and legislation aimed at meeting children's needs. The power this approach has created should be recognised. Those who use the rhetoric of children's needs do so in the context that those needs also exist within socio-cultural power frameworks. Children's rights movements seeking to protect children from harm must recognise the powerful impact of socio-cultural practices when policies aimed at children are enacted on the ground as well as ensuring that those with the power to construct policies are doing so in the most effective ways.

The need to address violence against women and girls

An example of one of the most intractable needs affecting children is the difficulty in addressing violence against women and girls (VAWG). While progress has been made in many areas, in a number of nations this remains a problem that has proved resistant to change despite intervention policies from international NGOs. A summary of evidence from 'What Works to Prevent Violence' (DFID, 2014a), a global programme aimed at building knowledge on how to prevent VAWG, used research evidence in low to middle income nations to draw conclusions on a number of intervention programmes (see Table 5.2).

The global programme discovered that small-scale, local interventions that addressed the need for protection against violence towards women and children were the most effective. However, careful monitoring is required if these are to be scaled up to national interventions or transferred into other nations. In addition, addressing VAWG requires long-term interventions to challenge the socio-cultural power structures in which abuse occurs. Empowering women and children and addressing gender discrimination in communities will require commitments beyond the span of usual development projects.

If the model of the *needy child* is useful to those in authority, it is worth considering what this means for the idea of children's agency. The discussion of children's needs suggests the *needy child* passively receives the help to meet those needs; seeing the child as an active agent in recognising their own needs challenges this approach somewhat. While the principle of participation rights suggests children's agency in recognising their own needs,

Table 5.2 *A summary of the evidence and research agenda for what works: A global programme to prevent violence against women and girls*

Effective interventions include:
• Microfinance and gender transformative approaches
• Group based relationship-level interventions
• Group education with community outreach (men/boys)
• Community mobilization – changing social norms
• Collectivisation and one-to-one interventions with vulnerable groups
• Alcohol reduction programmes
Promising interventions include:
• Parenting programmes
• Protection orders
• Shelters
• Whole-school interventions
• School based curriculum interventions
• Counselling, therapy and psychological support
• Transforming masculinities
Conflicting interventions include:
• Bystander interventions
• Perpetrators programmes
• Advocacy interventions
• Proactive arrests without protection orders
• Specialised courts
• Screening with referral in health facilities
• Sexual offenders registers

• Women's police stations/units
Ineffective interventions include:
• Routine screening for VAWG in health services
• Mandatory reporting and arrests for VAWG
• Single component communications campaigns

Source: DFID (2014b).

this does raise the interesting difference between *wants* and *needs*. The term *need* carries an emotive element missing from *want* (an idea not lost on many young children); *want*, arguably, removes the power away from the adult and towards the child. However, *want* also suggests individualism, the child as a consumer of goods. This materialistic aspect to *want* has become a concern in Western societies, particularly if it suggested that it impinges on children's well-being. The study of well-being is a relatively new area of research; the case study below considers the findings of UNICEF's research on the well-being of children in the 29 richest nations (UNICEF, 2013).

CASE STUDY

UNICEF (2013) Child Well-Being in Rich Countries: A Comparative Overview. Innocenti Report Card 11. Florence: UNICEF Office of Research.

In 2013 UNICEF reported an overall improvement in the well-being of children in 29 developed nations over the first decade of the twenty-first century. The Netherlands, Norway and Iceland ranked the highest for children's overall well-being. Five dimensions of children's lives were considered: material well-being, health and safety, education, behaviour and risks, and housing and environment. Four Nordic nations are at the top of the ranking, four Southern European nations are at the bottom and there is evidence that Central and Eastern European nations are closing the gap with more established nations. When children were asked to rate their well-being the rankings altered, with three of the Southern European nations jumping significantly up the rankings while a number of other European nations dropped, and the Netherlands remained at the top of the children's ranking. When asked, children rated relationships with family and friends as the most important factors to their sense of well-being.

The report showed a decrease in the number of children aged 11, 13 and 15 years who smoked, became pregnant, had experienced violence or bullying, or had used cannabis or alcohol in the majority of the nations. However, obesity showed an increase, and children's self-reported life satisfaction showed children in half the nations reporting a rise while children in the other half reported a decline in life satisfaction.

The report identifies the limitations to research aimed at measuring perceptions of well-being, not least the need for more child-orientated data such as the quality of parenting, children's mental and emotional health, children's exposure to domestic violence and the well-being of children under the care of the state. Most of the data relate to older children and young people. Another aspect to measuring well-being is the subjective/objective difference. The report combines both of these perspectives on well-being; however, self-reporting remains subject to some debate. Asking children to measure their own subjective views of well-being is arguably the most authentic measurement. A concern with self-reporting is the psychological aspect such as seeking peace of mind or aspirations which are possible or realistic. Nevertheless the report reflects the search to measure children's perspective of how they rate their own wants and needs.

Critical questions

It is important for those working with children and their families to also recognise the existence of power elements within their practice and how this impacts upon the approaches taken to meeting the needs of children and their families.

» *What evidence is there that policies in your area of practice make assumptions regarding children's needs, and why might this be?*

» *In your opinion, how can a non-ethnocentric stance be taken when considering children's needs in socio-cultural terms? Justify your answer.*

» *The report by DFID (2014b) suggested that small-scale local intervention actions were the most effective in battling VAWG. What power elements are likely to ensure this approach is expanded and what are likely to limit such interventions?*

» *When children were asked about their well-being in the UNICEF report they identified relationships with families and friends. How much consideration should policy-makers give to this when writing policies for children and families?*

Children's rights

At the start of this chapter children's rights were seen to fall within three broad strands: provision, protection and participation. Provision and protection can be seen to lie within what Wyness (2006) terms welfare rights, whereas participation lies within self-determination. Welfare rights have been shown to emerge from a history of social reform, with self-determination rights appearing in later contemporary understanding and, arguably, remain secondary to welfare rights.

Welfare rights are relational to the provision of children's needs and decisions regarding how they are met and by whom. The UNCRC presents two agents critical to the provision of welfare rights – the family and the state. As has been shown, this is not without significant challenges, not least the example of welfare rights that must compete with the domination of socio-cultural practices within families which lead to problems such as VAWG. Self-determination or participation rights (as evidenced in the UNCRC) are generally qualified by children's *evolving capacities*. The UNCRC does not define how participation rights are determined and leaves it for the state and families to decide, reflecting Bronfenbrenner and Morris's (1998) ecological approach to children's development which suggests that the child's social and cultural experiences within the family and wider society are highly influential on their general capacities. Children's self-determination rights require active listening and response by adults to the experiences of children and the choices they make.

Daiute (2008) reports how, in reality, this can both challenge adults who wish to protect children and also create opportunities to include the perspective and experiences of children in ways that can make welfare rights far more meaningful and relevant. Referring to a child who had grown up in a violent home explaining why she wanted to return to the armed insurgency group where she had worked as a medic (Sta. Maria, 2006), Daiute (2008) reflects on how the experiences of the child had led to *evolving capacities* in a way heavily influenced by violence both in her home and wider community, and the result was an ethical contradiction between her exercising self-determination rights in a manner that contravenes her welfare rights. Yet as the research on addressing VAWG demonstrates, such problems require small-scale interventions tailored to the needs of children within communities. The starting point for this is inevitably listening and responding to such experiences. A similar challenge is presented with child labour.

Child labour, like VAWG, has become an area of much concern for the protection of children and ensuring their rights. In 2010 the International Labour Organization (ILO) estimated that there were 215 million child labourers which actually reflects a gradual decline (ILO, 2010). For children, child labour contravenes children's right to free primary education (Article 28); it frequently contravenes children's right to protection from work that is harmful to their health (Article 32), the right to relax and play (Article 31) and governments' responsibility to help children in poverty (Article 26). Pressure has been placed on governments to strengthen legislation and abolish child labour. However, at times this sits at odds with children's self-determination rights and the right to respect their views (Article 12). Indeed for the poorest families, failure by states to support them means that child labour is necessitated by the need for survival. Abolishing child labour in such situations risks children entering more dangerous work. Indeed a great deal of child labour, particularly in rural areas, is domestic labour, mainly by girls, and is often considered an integral part of their role in the family (ILO, 2005). The case study below examines some of these issues based on research with child labourers in Ghana.

CASE STUDY

Okyere, S (2012) Are Working Children's Rights and Child Labour Abolition Complementary or Opposing Realms? International Social Work. 56 (1): pp 80–91.

Okyere interviewed a group of 57 children (30 girls and 27 boys) aged between 14 and 17 who were working at an artisanal gold mine in Ghana and he argues that it is the constraints on children's lives in the area that makes gold mining attractive work for the children. He argues that rather than simply abolishing child labour by preventing the children from working at the site, it is more effective to understand why children made these choices.

The site where Okyere based his research began following the removal of farmers from their lands to make way for a large gold mining organisation. Destitution led the farmers to take up this form of gold mining and they were then joined by others from around the country. Over 4000 men, women and children worked and lived on the site and although it was unhygienic and hazardous it was organised and had a committee which set strict rules and regulations. The children interviewed comprised local children and independent migrants from other parts of the country. Fifty of the children were either in school, had been in school or had completed compulsory education. Local children worked around school hours or at weekends, while others travelled to work at the site during school holidays. The work was highly gendered, giving girls less opportunities for different job roles than boys. The children were not employed by others and could work when they wanted. Okyere saw no evidence that the children handled toxic materials such as mercury or that they were involved in sex work and none of the children reported any maltreatment or abuse. The committee had strict rules on the hours people worked, including the children, and that male and female workers received the same pay which was fixed, meaning the children knew what they would earn at the end of the day. That said, the work had potential health and safety hazards for the children and it was not the children's preference to do such work.

Okyere reinforces that work is an integral part of African childhoods which, combined with poverty, influence child labour. However, the deciding factor the children gave for working was their desire to be able to support themselves through their education and to be able to access health care. While education upto 15 years of age is free in Ghana, parents must still provide school uniforms and equipment, which makes education inaccessible for impoverished families. Working on the gold mining site offered the children an opportunity to earn good levels of money quickly in order that they could also attend school.

For these children, and others on the site, work offered them the opportunity to continue their education; however, working while studying also jeopardised their chances of completing school, meaning the money and work could be wasted. One 16-year-old boy reported that he was already the oldest in his class and he had taken two months off school to work, meaning a further setback in his education. Of the children, 80 per cent also supported their families and relatives with their earnings, while some lived alone and worked to support themselves. All the children reported that they had not been pressurised by parents or family to work and were doing so *freely*, although Okyere questions how *free* they were to make this choice given their severely limited options.

Okyere concludes that the stance taken by NGOs such as UNICEF and the ILO to abolish child labour, even as a result of poverty, in such industries represents a totalitarian approach which would reduce the children's options still further. Okyere argues that the children were not accessing their rights to education, relaxation and play, not as a result of child labour but as a result of failures to uphold these rights by those in authority. While the NGOs seek to remove the hazards of child labour from the lives of these children, Okyere argues the hazards of poverty were what really needed to be addressed as the work offered the children a solution to these very real problems. Recognising the real risk of child slavery and abuse, Okyere demonstrates that organisations also need to find ways to respond to work as a necessary option for these children, and their right to have their views respected.

It can be argued that denying these children the right to work would not be in their best interests; what they require is their government to take its responsibility to ensure their right of support for their families, to enable them to access their rights to education and relaxation and play. This case study demonstrates the complex nature of the child rights agenda when it is being enacted in the real world and also the importance of recognising that self-determination rights need to be responded to.

Critical questions

» How do the contradictions that can occur between welfare and self-determination rights impact upon practitioners working with children and families?

» What are the implications of studies such as the one above for the child rights agenda?

» Develop an argument that analyses the different sources of power that influence the balance between welfare and self-determination rights?

» Does the child rights agenda support children to recognise their responsibilities for others or not? Justify your argument.

Critical reflections

This chapter has examined the relationship between children's rights and children's needs. By doing so it has considered some of the key challenges that arise when children's needs are analysed in terms of their socio-cultural element particularly in a global context, which led to an examination of the challenges facing the push to eradicate VAWG. The power that is created by the idea of need leads us to examine how needs are identified, measured and addressed, and by whom. The idea of a needy child challenges us to reflect on children's ideas of what they want and need and to consider children's experiences of well-being.

Children's rights have become an integral part of the study of international childhoods. This chapter reflected that the child rights agenda, as seen in charters such as the UNCRC and the ACRWC, presents a general division between welfare and self-determination rights which can lead to contradictions and difficulties. The analysis of the different rights involved in the analysis of child labour gave an opportunity to consider some of these contradictions in real terms.

Further reading

Committee on the Rights of the Child. Available at: www.ohchr.org/EN/HRBodies/CRC/Pages/CRCIndex.aspx

Department for International Development (DFID). Available at: https://www.gov.uk/government/organisations/department-for-international-development

The African Charter on the Rights and Welfare of the Child. Available at: www.acerwc.org

References

ACRWC (1990) African Charter on the Rights and Welfare of the Child. [online] Available at: http://acerwc.org/wp-content/uploads/2011/04/ACRWC-EN.pdf (accessed 28 July 2014).

Bronfenbrenner, U and Morris P (1998) The Ecology of Developmental Processes, in Damon, W and Lerner, R (eds) *Handbook of Child Psychology: Theoretical Models of Human Development. Volume 1*. New York: Wiley.

Bühler-Niederberger, D (2003) The Needy Child and the Naturalization of Politics: Political Debate in Germany, in Hallett, C and Prout, A (eds) *Hearing the Voices of Children*. Abingdon: Routledge.

Daiute, C (2008) The Rights of Children, the Rights of Nations: Developmental Theory and the Politics of Children's Rights. *Journal of Social Issues*. 64 (4): pp 701–723.

DFID (2014a) Funding for What Works to Prevent Violence Against Women and Girls. [online] Available at: https://www.gov.uk/funding-for-what-works-to-prevent-violence-against-women-and-girls (accessed 30 July 2014).

DFID (2014b) A Summary of the Evidence and Research Agenda for What Works: A Global Programme to Prevent Violence against Women and Girls. [online] Available at: https://www.gov.uk/government/uploads/system/uploads/attachment_data/file/337599/summary-evidence-research-agenda-C.pdf (accessed 30 July 2014).

Fuchs, E (2008) Children's Rights and Global Civil Society. *Comparative Education*. 43 (3): pp 398–412.

Hall, D (2005) Children, Rights, and Responsibilities. *Archives of Disease in Childhood*. 90: pp 171–173.

International Labour Organization (2005) *Good Practices and Lessons Learned on Child and Adolescent Domestic Labour in Central America and the Dominican Republic: A Gender Perspective*. San José: ILO.

International Labour Organization (2010) *Facts on Child Labour 2010*. Geneva: ILO.

Okyere, S (2012) Are Working Children's Rights and Child Labour Abolition Complementary or Opposing Realms? *International Social Work*. 56 (1): pp 80–91.

Sta.Maria, M (2006) Paths to Filipino Youth Involvement in Violent Conflict, in Daiute, C, Beykont, Z, Higson-Smith, C and Nucci, L (eds) *International Perspectives on Youth Conflict and Development*. New York: Oxford University Press.

UN (1959) Declaration of the Rights of the Child. [online] Available at: www.un.org (accessed 24 July 2014).

UN (1989) The United Nations Convention on the Rights of the Child. [online] Available at: http://www.unicef.org.uk/Documents/Publication-pdfs/UNCRC_PRESS200910web.pdf (accessed 16 March 2015).

UNICEF (2013) Child Well-Being in Rich Countries: A Comparative Overview. *Innocenti Report Card 11*. Florence: UNICEF Office of Research.

Woodhead, M (1997) Psychology and the Cultural Construction of Children's Needs, in James, A and Prout, A (eds) *Constructing and Reconstructing Childhood*. Abingdon: Routledge.

Wyness, M (2006) *Childhood and Society: An Introduction to the Sociology of Childhood*. Basingstoke: Palgrave Macmillan.

6   Children's health and welfare

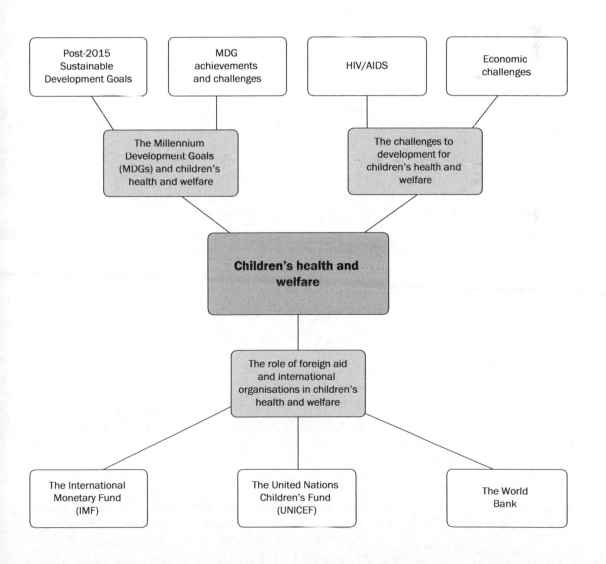

> *In order to survive and develop to their full potential, children need health care, nutritious food, education that nurtures their minds and equips them with useful knowledge and skills, freedom from violence and exploitation, and the time and space to play.*
>
> (UNICEF, 2014, p 5)

Introduction

As the quote above demonstrates, an examination of children's health and welfare requires the consideration of a number of separate facets which actively combine to generate positive or negative outcomes. A global perspective considers how judgements and decisions made about these facets of children's lives influence their health and welfare. Chapter 7 examines the impact of inequalities, both within and between nations, on childhoods, including children's welfare. This chapter focuses on what is meant by children's health and welfare and who and what have the greatest influences on those facets that UNICEF identify as necessary for positive outcomes in children's lives.

The terms health and welfare have now become such ubiquitous terms that they are seldom examined and questioned. However, as Chapter 5's examination of children's needs demonstrated, it is important to be willing to scrutinise the language used within discourses.

Defining children's health and welfare

- In 1948, the World Health Organization (WHO) agreed the definition of health as: '*a state of complete physical, mental and social well-being and not merely the absence of disease or infirmity*' (WHO, 1946, p 100), a definition which they have not altered since. This presents a highly personalised micro level view of health which is likely to fluctuate not only between individuals but also within an individual person's lifetime.

- Public health, however, refers to more meso level, organised measures taken to promote health, prevent disease and prolong the life of a population as a whole and does not focus on individual people or diseases (WHO, 2014).

- Global health recognises the important consequences of taking a broader view beyond national borders to macro level perspectives of health. Indeed as Ehiri (2009) argues, examining global health offers important lessons on the commonality of managing health challenges in wealthy and less wealthy nations and the need for co-operation that transcends national borders.

It is this broader view of health which UNICEF reflects at the start of the chapter and, as this chapter demonstrates, it has become a rallying point for NGOs to particularly focus on the health and welfare of children globally. It is this view that enables the analysis of powerful influences in this chapter.

Defining welfare is similarly challenging, it is commonly seen in micro level terms as personal well-being or in meso and macro level economic terms as the requirement for financial support from a state or international organisation. Therefore, welfare can arguably be considered from an economic or sociological viewpoint. In economic terms, welfare can be seen in relation to goods and services which influence well-being and the distribution of wealth. From a global perspective this frequently sees data that connect a nation's economy to the standard of living for its population and is often expressed as a nation's per capita GDP, namely the gross domestic product of a nation divided by the number in the population. A more subtle measure now used is the Gini coefficient (sometimes referred to as the Gini index) which measures inequality within a nation in economic terms by seeing how the wealth of a nation is distributed across the population. This takes a measure where 0 equals complete equality and 1 complete inequality (one person has all the income, all the others have none). This leads to the challenge of considering the boundary between the responsibility of a nation's government, the international community, NGOs and the individual.

In sociological terms welfare is often linked to well-being; however, whereas well-being often holds broader reference to less tangible aspects such as realising potential and mental health (WHO, 2013), welfare is more closely related to meeting the essential physical needs of individuals and families and is therefore subject to change. Greve (2008) suggests that as nations become wealthier the link between income and welfare in terms of a sense of well-being cannot be guaranteed over time. This makes judging welfare in sociological terms across a population difficult. Whereas the opportunities available to individuals to meet their essential needs can be considered in sociological terms as well as economic terms, individuals will also make choices which might impact their welfare in the short or long term. For example, we have seen that the long-term welfare of a child is frequently linked to that child attending school to gain an education. However, the opportunities to do so can be impacted upon by economic factors, such as poverty, or sociological factors, such as the value a community places on education, but there is also the child's individual choice about their engagement in education. As the case study in Chapter 5 considering child labour demonstrated, children can also be active agents in attempting to attend to their own individual welfare and that of their families. In economic and sociological terms welfare is not easily defined and can mean different things when considered on a broad national level, and on the smaller micro level it is frequently linked with the less tangible ideas of well-being. This complexity should be remembered when studying issues of welfare.

Critical questions

»   *What is your opinion of the facets relating to children's health and welfare identified in the quote at the start of the chapter?*

»   *Why is it important to examine definitions of health and welfare when studying children, families and childhood?*

»   *What are the implications of these different definitions on the way you approach children and families in your practice?*

»   *Consider a health issue for children in your practice. Explain how taking a global view of health might help address this issue for children in the United Kingdom. How might it limit the way this issue is addressed?*

This chapter is divided into three parts:

1.   the role of foreign aid and international organisations in children's health and welfare;

2.   the Millennium Development Goals (MDGs) and children's health and welfare;

3.   the challenges to development for children's health and welfare.

The role of foreign aid and international organisations in children's health and welfare

Much of the discussion in this chapter is linked to human development and how children's health and welfare is heavily influenced not only by the decisions of families and governments but also by the decisions of international organisations. The most influential of these is the United Nations, with numerous programmes and institutes relevant to children's health and development globally. Three of these are considered here: the UNICEF, the World Bank and the IMF; their influence is evidenced primarily through the provision of aid, financial and social, in order to meet the health and welfare needs of nations.

The role of foreign aid in addressing the problems of nations is not without challenges; the main challenge being how a shift of focus onto trade rather than aid would be more beneficial. Arguably, if instead of the provision of loans and aid, trade were made more equitable for low income nations this would better support the economies of developing nations (Moyo, 2010). Nevertheless, foreign aid and financial support remain the chief means by which support for children's health and welfare in developing nations is managed. The problems that harm children's health and welfare are complex and multifaceted, influenced by factors such as a nation's social and economic stability, the governance of welfare systems and the natural environment. This means any system aimed at supporting children's health and welfare will be slow moving with positive outcomes only likely to emerge from long-term solutions for recipient nations (Arndt et al, 2009).

The United Nations Children's Fund (UNICEF)

Examining children's health and welfare must consider children's rights in identifying children's health and welfare needs. Chapter 5 identified the complexities of children's rights and the role UNICEF plays in identifying and overseeing the international provision of these rights. UNICEF was created in 1946 and is mandated by the United Nations General Assembly to advocate for the protection of children's rights, meet their basic needs and expand opportunities for them to reach their full potential (UNICEF, 2013). Its non-partisan approach, which targets the most disadvantaged children, has made it one of the most highly regarded international NGOs working with children, particularly because of its willingness to deliver humanitarian support in emergencies, whether from conflict or natural disasters. In 1988 UNICEF established the Innocenti Research Centre in Florence to support its advocacy and to research current and future arees for its work and it has become a useful source of international research on children's health and welfare. (See Further Reading for links to Innocenti Research Centre.)

One of the main activities of UNICEF is its collection, compilation, analysis and dissemination of data regarding the monitoring of children's rights, health and welfare. UNICEF keeps a global database which is updated to produce an annual review, 'The State of the World's Children'. This data is used to report trends and data-driven policies (Murray and Newby, 2012), but predominantly the data enables agencies to monitor whether targets for programmes are being met in individual nations and internationally. The data is collected on nations from high to low income, although the collection systems differ as the industrialised nations do not have UNICEF field offices but do have national administrative records and census data. Accurate and timely data remains a challenge as it is a crucial part of development programmes, particularly in order that organisations such as the World Bank and the IMF, responsible for calculating the financial costs of these programmes, can make useful budget predictions.

All this has resulted in UNICEF becoming one of the most influential international organisations in shaping not only policies on the provision of aid to children but also in shaping ideas about childhood in the majority world (Penn, 2005). Its rights-based approach has led it to focus on universal values which at times can sit at odds with the experiences of children within individual nations (see Chapter 5 on the discussion and a case study on child labour).

However, UNICEF is not without its critics. UNICEF's stance on the role of contraception for reproductive health and the spread of HIV/AIDS, for example, has led to criticism by some religious groups, particularly in the United States. UNICEF itself has reported weaknesses in its perceived reluctance to criticise governments over their policies and practices with children (UNICEF, 2004). In recent years, UNICEF, like many other NGOs such as the Red Cross and the Red Crescent, has developed partnerships with large multinational corporations in what have become known as business–humanitarian partnerships (BHPs). UNICEF has partnerships with large multinational companies such as Proctor and Gamble and Unilever. While this has the positive effect of developing corporate responsibilities, social justice and legitimacy for these large companies, it is not without its dilemmas. The main concerns of BHPs are usually around the lack of accountability, ethical safeguarding and issues such as the use of emblems and product endorsement (Andonova and Carbonnier, 2014). However, BHPs offer not just sponsorship but also equipment, services and skills which can be utilised by UNICEF and national governments. Indeed working in partnership with governments on a financial level to resolve problems has become the particular domain of two of the UN's specialised agencies, the World Bank and the IMF.

The World Bank

The World Bank Group began functioning in 1946; the World Bank is a component of this group and is composed of the International Bank for Reconstruction and Development (IBRD) – which finances debts – and the International Development Association (IDA) – which provides interest free loans or grants. The World Bank claims two goals – to end extreme poverty in a generation and to boost shared prosperity (World Bank, 2014). Through the IBRD and the IDA, the World Bank focuses on low income developing nations in a wide range of areas from human development such as health and education to infrastructure such as roads and large industrial construction projects. It provides loans to its 187 member nations as well as grants to the poorest nations; in 2012 it lent US$35 billion. (See Further Reading for more information on the activities of the World Bank.)

The World Bank liaises with NGOs on projects which tend to be agreed between the World Bank and national governments. However, for organisations such as the World Bank, agreeing on the amount of funding that is required is complex. Schäferhoff et al (2010) noted that this has been made more difficult when different models are used to calculate how much money is required to fund assistance programmes. Looking at how budgets are calculated for financing maternal and child health for nations that were struggling to meet their targets (see later in this chapter for an examination of the Millennium Development Goals), Schäferhoff et al (2010) found that even within the UN different organisations used different methods for calculating the cost of financing programmes. While this problem has been recognised and the UN is working on developing a unified model for calculating the cost of health and welfare programmes, it does raise two important points about how to manage global health and welfare. First collecting data on child health and welfare problems internationally is complicated, and if it is to be useful then it needs to be both timely and accurate if organisations such as the World Bank are to accurately identify the cost of financing programmes to manage problems. The second point is that even if the data is accurate and timely, the way the costs are calculated needs to be consistent between the large international organisations if they are to be able to make accurate budget predictions in order that the costs of meeting health and welfare needs of children are clear.

The World Bank is frequently subject to severe criticism; not least that taking approaches to global economics that favour capitalism actually causes global inequality, as the most powerful nations have the greatest influences over the World Bank which leads to decisions that favour Western approaches to the global economy. This criticism is demonstrated in the voting rights of individual nations within the World Bank – the nations which make the highest donations hold the most voting rights, with the United States, Japan, the United Kingdom, Germany, France and China holding the highest (World Bank, 2014a). The approaches taken by the World Bank are shared with its partner UN organisation, the IMF, with both organisations frequently co-operating on actions.

The International Monetary Fund (IMF)

Formed in 1945, the IMF was created to ensure a framework for international economic co-operation. Today it advises governments on their economies, provides loans to nations in economic difficulties and provides technical assistance to nations in managing their economies through collaboration with the World Bank, other UN organisations and international institutions (IMF, 2014). Unlike the World Bank, IMF loans are used to stabilise currencies, pay for imports and restore a nation's economic growth. As the World Bank is engaged in poverty management, the two organisations frequently work together. (See Further Reading for more information on the current activities of the IMF.) The current global economic crisis has led to greater involvement of the IMF in creating multilateral agreements on managing the economies of some of the world's poorest nations which suffered the most. It is the poorest communities within those nations that bear the greatest impact of the economic crises, and within those communities it is the women and children who are most vulnerable (see Chapter 7, women as social *shock absorbers*).

However, the way the IMF makes its recommendations and gives its advice is subject to some degree of criticism. There is the charge that the advice can be inaccurate, favour particular capitalist models or can lead to political change within nations when governments use the IMF advice to push through their own political agendas without full democratic discussion (Woods, 2006).

The problems of organisations such as the World Bank and the IMF funding health and welfare systems in developing nations is that the models used do not necessarily reflect the deeply entrenched problems within those nations. The case study below considers a review of the approaches taken to universal health care initiatives in India and the unintended impact upon the poorest families.

CASE STUDY

Nayar, K (2013) Universalizing Health Services in India: The Techno-managerial Fix. Indian Journal of Public Health. *57 (4): pp 248–253.*

In this review of universal approaches to health services in India, Nayar suggests that NGOs and international institutions such as the World Bank have created a discourse that problems with health and health services in nations such as India are the result of government inefficiency. This has led to these organisations promoting a reduction in the role of the state in health services and increasing the role of private organisations. Nayar argues that these are external pressures which mean programmes are managed in ways that do not help India to develop a workable welfare state. These include programmes aimed at providing community health centres which suffered from a lack of trained staff and a model transferred from China to train a member of the community to deal with basic health issues which were not effective within Indian society because of the hierarchical caste system. The latest programme is the National Rural Health Mission which combines public and private health systems.

Pressure from NGOs to reach targets for specific health activities, such as immunisation programmes, combined with advice from organisations such as the IMF and World Bank for managing the economy, Nayar argues, do not tackle the main problems that face India. Inequality in Indian society and the lack of infrastructure to be able to implement the plans and strategies of external organisations are major factors in addressing the health of Indian society. His suggestion is that if a working health care system is to be developed then it needs to see the problems of India in a more holistic manner. Rather than seeing health as something separate to the wider problems in society that are detrimental to people's health, Nayar reasons for an approach which focuses on tackling the wider social problems that impact on the health of the poorest families.

Critical questions

» Having used the further readings to examine the roles of international organisations and NGOs, what is your opinion of their role in global health and welfare initiatives?

» What motives, in your opinion, influence the function of these international organisations? Justify your answers.

» What conclusions can you draw from the case study about how international organisations influence the health and welfare of children in low income nations such as India?

» What have been the unforeseen impacts of government health initiatives upon the children and families in your practice?

The Millennium Development Goals and children's health and welfare

The United Nations Millennium Declaration adopted in September 2000 saw the nations of the UN make a fresh commitment to a set of values, principles and objectives for the twenty-first century (United Nations, 2000) based upon peace, development and human rights. The United Nations Millennium Development Goals (MDGs) became the tools by which development was to be achieved. The MDGs, further broken down into targets and indicators, have been the most widely supported systems that have come to dominate development for the past two decades. The 8 goals and 18 targets have become the framework for development aimed at confronting poverty, hunger, education, gender inequality, maternal and child mortality, communicable disease, the environment and global partnership (see Table 6.1)

Table 6.1 The Millennium Development Goals

Goal 1: Eradicate extreme hunger and poverty
Goal 2: Achieve universal primary education
Goal 3: Promote gender equality and empower women
Goal 4: Reduce child mortality
Goal 5: Improve maternal health
Goal 6: Combat HIV/AIDS, malaria and other disease
Goal 7: Ensure environmental sustainability
Goal 8: Global partnership for development

The eight goals comprise targets and indicators which are used to measure progress, with adaptations to the targets for individual nations (see Further Reading for more information). Since their construction in 2000, and following their adoption by the United Nations Assembly (United Nations, 2014a), the MDGs have become the context in which international development has been organised. The 189 UN member states agreed to work towards meeting these goals by 2015 through a series of action plans and funding which recognise the interconnectedness between the goals. Since 2000, monitoring and tracking of the goals means it is possible to measure the achievements both globally and for individual nations in meeting the targets set (see Further Reading for MDG indicators and achievements).

MDG achievements and challenges

As the 2015 deadline arrives, significant achievements have been made particularly with regard to hunger and extreme poverty (MDG 1) and enrolment of girls into primary school (MDG 2). Governments have been held to account for their efforts in development through the monitoring systems. As individual nations were made accountable for the data that was regularly presented on meeting these targets, the level of responsibilities placed on governments led to increased commitment to development. For example, Mukonka et al (2014) report that in Zambia, holding a country countdown to progress on achieving MDG 4 (reducing child mortality) and MDG 5 (improving maternal health) had a positive impact nationally. The conference was able to raise awareness of bottlenecks in areas that were impacting negatively on child and maternal health, share good practice, improve training and legislation on the roles and responsibilities of midwives and gain commitment from government health officials on their responsibilities towards the population's health.

However, these successes have been imbalanced when compared across individual nations. Much of the poverty reduction has been attributed to the economic growth of nations such as China and India, while severe poverty continues to be a problem in parts of sub-Saharan Africa, with inequalities also emerging within nations particularly between urban and rural communities (Bourguignon et al, 2008). Lomazzi et al (2014) identify that, while significant progress has been achieved from the MDGs, some of the greatest challenges they faced came from the fact that the targets were not sufficiently comprehensive, with some considered too narrow. It was argued that this led to a focus on those targets most easily achieved and the consequent uneven spread of success. This approach created *development silos* where programmes become absorbed on achieving a particular goal without recognising the wider issues which impact upon it. This lack of recognition of how social, economic and environmental factors influence the achievement of the goals, as the case study earlier in this chapter demonstrated, meant the emphasis on success with the MDG targets did not necessarily take sufficient account of the social complications which impacted on them (Stuckler et al, 2010). One of the greatest criticisms has been the lack of recognition of the impact of gender inequality in achieving all the MDGs, not just MDG 3 but also as a human rights based issue. Sen and Mukherjee (2014), for example, contend that failure to recognise women's autonomy and agency is likely to have slowed down success in the MDGs, and it needs to be one of the main considerations to the post-2015 development agenda.

Post-2015 Sustainable Development Goals

In 2012 the UN Secretary General commissioned a high level panel to advise on a global development framework post-2015. In July 2014 the UN General Assembly Open Working Group submitted its proposal for a set of goals for the General Assembly to consider in September 2015. These consisted of 17 Sustainable Development Goals (SDGs) (see Table 6.2) that aim to include economic, social and environmental dimensions.

Table 6.2 *Proposed Sustainable Development Goals*

Goal 1: End poverty in all its forms everywhere
Goal 2: End hunger, achieve food security and improved nutrition, and promote sustainable agriculture
Goal 3: Ensure healthy lives and promote well-being for all at all ages
Goal 4: Ensure inclusive and equitable quality education and promote life-long learning opportunities for all
Goal 5: Achieve gender equality and empower all women and girls
Goal 6: Ensure availability and sustainable management of water and sanitation for all
Goal 7: Ensure access to affordable, reliable, sustainable, and modern energy for all
Goal 8: Promote sustained, inclusive and sustainable economic growth, full and productive employment and decent work for all
Goal 9: Build resilient infrastructure, promote inclusive and sustainable industrialisation and foster innovation
Goal 10: Reduce inequality within and among countries
Goal 11: Make cities and human settlements inclusive, safe, resilient and sustainable
Goal 12: Ensure sustainable consumption and production patterns
Goal 13: Take urgent action to combat climate change and its impacts
Goal 14: Conserve and sustainably use the oceans, seas and marine resources for sustainable development
Goal 15: Protect, restore and promote sustainable use of terrestrial ecosystems, sustainably manage forests, combat desertification, and halt and reverse land degradation and halt biodiversity loss
Goal 16: Promote peaceful and inclusive societies for sustainable development, provide access to justice for all and build effective, accountable and inclusive institutions at all levels
Goal 17: Strengthen the means of implementation and revitalise the global partnership for sustainable development

Source: UN, 2014a.

The formulation of the SDGs follows a significantly different course to the MDGs. The development of the SDGs has been a far more collaborative process with UN-led thematic consultations and individual national discussions. Thematic discussions considered 11 issues ranging from inequalities, health and education to population dynamics and involved stakeholders and interested parties. The national discussions took place in 88 countries with the aim of encouraging a global active participation prior to final agreements of the SDGs. (See Further Reading for the dialogues on the post-2015 SDGs.)

The global situation also differs from the one which existed when the MDGs were created. The majority of the world's poor now live in middle income nations. The economic situation globally has altered following the economic crises of 2008; there has been a rise in the role of digital technology and communications, and the climate change agenda has become more important (Brolan et al, 2014). However, an issue that remains is the relationship between development agendas and the political arena, particularly with regard to the provision of development aid for nations with political regimes which fail to meet the needs of their populations. The case study below examines the impact on child and maternal mortality rates in two nations as a result of international sanctions that have reduced the flow of aid.

CASE STUDY

Grundy, J, Bowen, K, Annear, P and Biggs, B (2012) The Responsibility to Protect: Inequities in International Aid Flows to Myanmar and the Democratic People's Republic of Korea and Their Impact on Maternal and Child Health. Asian Studies Review. *36: pp 171–187*

The Union of Myanmar (also known as Burma) and the Democratic People's Republic of Korea (DPRK) are the most disadvantaged aid recipients in Asia. In this study the authors analyse how the inequities in the movement of international aid to these nations have impacted upon maternal and child mortality rates. Problems of unequal global health are often related to failures to implement health systems in nations, natural disasters, conflicts and disease outbreaks which all lead to international co-operation, or *global health diplomacy*, in an attempt to address the problems. However, the authors argue that more *silent* health problems such as malnutrition and maternal and child mortality do not receive the same recognition, and this is particularly so in nations such as Myanmar and the DPRK. International foreign policy aimed at bringing about regime changes in these two nations have not been successful, but these policies have instead exacerbated the chronic problems in the health systems and for the vulnerable populations, predominantly women and children.

Myanmar has been governed by military rule for over 40 years and while moves are being made towards civilian democracy, the military remain in control with very low levels of spending on health and welfare for the population. The maternal health care services suffer from low investment, lack of midwives and basic equipment, particularly in rural areas. The flow of aid to Myanmar has been patchy and reflects the stances of different governments to the military regime, although this is improving with the progress to democratic rule.

The highly centralised nation of the DPRK suffered severe drought in the 1990s, and while it has a well-resourced health workforce and system, there is a general lack of basic resources nationally, meaning that in the winter there is little heating and there is a shortage of medicines and drug supplies which impact heavily on the maternal death rates. The DPRK has no access to international loans; in addition, the isolation of health staff from participating in international technical developments and training has a negative impact when combined with economic sanctions and diplomacy strategies aimed at encouraging the nation's denuclearisation.

Declarations such as the UNCRC and the MDGs make the access to health care a fundamental right for children. While this is primarily the responsibility of individual national governments, from an international perspective responsibility also lies with the international community, particularly when the nation is considered to have failed in its duty. However, the authors demonstrate that the flow of aid to Myanmar and the DPRK is considerably less than to other nations in the region despite both nations having some of the lowest reductions in maternal and under-five child mortality rates. The combination of little development aid from international agencies and low levels of investment from the governments have had a severe effect on the health and mortality rates of women and children in these two nations.

The study reveals the inability of the national governments and the international community to ensure the rights of the women and children and their entitlement to basic life-saving health provision, and this leads the authors to query whose responsibility it is to protect the population in such circumstances and how. The authors argue that the most successful, equitable interventions *encourage* and *help* nations to exercise their responsibility to protect the population through a shared responsibility between the individual nations and the international community. The study suggests strategies for this such as targeting aid at human security by exempting food security, health and education from political sanctions against a state and analysing the impact of foreign and defence policies on the public health of the nation targeted.

Critical questions

»   *What choices would you have made to ensure effective strategies were in place for the MDGs to meet the health and welfare needs of children?*

»   *What recommendations would you make to the SDGs for children's health and welfare?*

»   *What would be the challenges to implementing the equitable development strategies discussed in the case study?*

»   *Compare the experiences of women and children in Myanmar and the DPRK against the expectations of the UNCRC, MDGs and SDGs. How would you prioritise a more equitable approach to aid development and international politics?*

The challenges to development for children's health and welfare

HIV/AIDS

The earlier section described how ensuring that provision of aid reaches the children and families most in need is a particular challenge globally. Chapter 3 confirmed HIV/AIDS has had a serious detrimental influence on the health and welfare of children and families. MDG 6 (combat HIV/AIDS, malaria and other disease) reflected this concern; however, within the post-2015 development agenda there is currently no specific provision regarding HIV/AIDS or other communicable diseases, and it is instead consumed within SDG 3 (ensure healthy lives and promote well-being for all at all ages), although there will remain national health targets to achieve quality health care, aimed at enabling populations to hold governments to account. Chapter 3 considered how HIV/AIDS has led to the emergence of child-headed households in parts of Africa. While recognising the resilience and agency many of these children are called upon to use in such situations, they vividly illustrate the ongoing challenges from this disease.

Recognition of the risks from HIV/AIDS led to an unprecedented international drive to tackle its effect and reduce its spread. The development of affordable antiretroviral treatment (ART) has had a considerable impact in high HIV-prevalent regions. So too has the development of health schemes which limit the transmission of HIV from mothers to babies. Indeed Natrass (2014) contends that these two drives alone have helped with achieving MDGs 4 and 5 (maternal and child health) in areas particularly affected by HIV/AIDS.

However, despite these successes, post-2015 SDGs need to face the challenges that continue to be posed from the disease, particularly as middle income nations will be expected to take a greater responsibility for management and finance of HIV/AIDS policies. The treatment of the disease is no longer an *emergency* but has become a chronic, long-term, rights-based issue with the continued need for ART, mother to baby transmission prevention and information on preventing new infections through sexual health education that will need to be combined with other health demands. This is in addition to tackling the ongoing welfare support required for children and young people orphaned by the disease.

Economic challenges

The economic cost of delivering the MDGs is unclear; however, Bryce et al (2005) estimate the cost of delivering specific child survival interventions at approximately US$5.1 billion annually. Atisophon et al (2011) estimate the cost of achieving the first six MDGs at US$120 billion annually. The calculation of these estimates of cost are complicated. Atisophon et al (2011) acknowledge they are influenced by a number of factors including their use as a means of gaining increased foreign aid and that there is a risk of *double counting* as the drop in child mortality rates, for example, influence the cost of health provision and education. As Atisophon et al (2011, p 48) point out *'financing health and education expenditures is not identical to ensuring health and education outcomes'*. Post-2015 the cost of financing children's health and welfare will require expenditure at all levels of government if target setting is to be successful with the SDGs.

A second issue with calculating the cost of development is the delay and, at times, inaccuracies of data, both from the recipient nations and from the donor nations. This makes it difficult to track the contributions from donors and the data on targets from the recipient nations. This is particularly a problem as both the MDGs and the SDGs are target-led which requires accurate data to ensure that goals are working effectively.

Critical questions

» What is your opinion of the challenges facing global development for children's health and welfare post-2015?

» Research the work being done to support the health and welfare needs of the children in a majority world nation. How are the policies being implemented likely to address the long-term impact of HIV/AIDS on the health and welfare of children in this nation?

» What conclusions can you draw from the economic challenges to funding the health and welfare of children post-2015? Justify your answer.

Critical reflections

This chapter has examined the importance of taking a broader view of children's health and welfare globally. This has stretched beyond national borders to explore the international organisations that influence the approaches taken which impact upon the lives of millions of children globally. The issues are great and the solutions complicated and uncertain. However, the role of development targets in terms of development and the use of goals have become the dominant approach to addressing the needs and welfare of these children.

At times these organisations and approaches can seem remote from the lived experiences of those in high income nations. Yet having an understanding of these organisations enables us to not only gain a wider understanding of childhoods globally but also recognise the experiences that children who are refugees or asylum seekers are likely to bring with them. This becomes a means to recognise the connections that exist between different nations. As practitioners working with children and families, it is important to recognise that globalisation in communications now makes it possible to contact these organisations in order to support our own professional development and for sharing information and good practice.

Further reading

Dialogues on the post-2015 SDGs. Information is available at: www.worldwewant2015.org/sitemap#thematic

IMF. Information on its current focus of activity is available at: www.imf.org

Innocenti Research Centre. Information on current research is available at: www.unicef-irc.org

MDG. Information on the history of the goals and targets is available at: www.un.org/millenniumgoals/bkgd.shtml

MDG indicators. Information on the progress being made globally and by individual nations to meeting the MDG targets is available at: http://mdgs.un.org/unsd/mdg/

The World Bank. Information on the current activities is available at: www.worldbank.org

References

Andonova, L and Carbonnier, G (2014) Business–Humanitarian Partnerships: Processes of Normative Legitimation. *Globalizations*. 11 (3): pp 349–367.

Arndt, C, Jones, S and Tarp, F (2009) Aid and Growth: Have We Come Full Circle? Discussion Paper No. 2009/05. UNU-WIDER.

Atisophon, V, Bueren, J, De Paepe, G, Garroway, C and Stijns, J (2011) Revisiting MDG Cost Estimates From a Domestic Resource Mobilisation Perspective. Working Paper No. 306. Paris: OECD.

Bourguignon, F, Bénassy-Quéré, A, Dercon, S, Estache, A, Gunning, J, Kanbur, R, Klasen, S, Maxwell, S, Platteau, J and Spadaro, A (2008) Millennium Development Goals at Midpoint: Where Do We Stand and Where Do We Need to Go? European Report on Development. Brussels: European Commission.

Brolan, C, Lee, S, Kim, D and Hill, P (2014) Back to the Future: What Would the Post-2015 Global Development Goals Look Like if We Replicated Methods Used to Construct the Millennium Development Goals? *Globalization and Health*. 10 (19) [online] Available at: www.globalizationandhealth.com/content/10/1/19 (accessed 7 August 2014).

Bryce, J, Black, R, Walker, N, Bhutta, Z, Lawn, J and Steketee, R (2005) Can the World Afford to Save the Lives of 6 Million Children Each Year? *Lancet*. 365: pp 2193–2200.

Ehiri, J (ed) (2009) *Maternal and Child Health: Global Challenges, Programs, and Policies*. New York: Springer.

Greve, B (2008) What Is Welfare? *Central European Journal of Public Policy*. 2 (1): pp 50–73.

Grundy, J, Bowen, K, Annear, P and Biggs, B (2012) The Responsibility to Protect: Inequities in International Aid Flows to Myanmar and the Democratic People's Republic of Korea and their Impact on Maternal and Child Health. *Asian Studies Review*. 36: pp 171–187.

IMF (2014) About the IMF. [online] Available at: www.imf.org/external/about.htm (accessed 6 August 2014).

Lomazzi, M, Borisch, B and Laaser, U (2014) The Millennium Development Goals: Experiences, Achievements and What's Next? *Global Health Action*. **7**: 23695 [online] Available at: http://dx.doi.org/10.3402/gha.v7.23695 (accessed 7 August 2014).

Moyo, D (2010) *Dead Aid: Why Aid Is Not Working and how there is another way for Africa*. London: Penguin.

Mukonka, V, Malumo, S, Kalesha, P, Namboa, M, Mwale, R, Mwinga, K, Katepa-Bwalya, M, Babaniyi, O, Mason, E, Phiri, C and Wamulme, P (2014) Holding a Country Countdown to 2015 Conference on Millennium Development Goals (MDGs) – The Zambian Experience. *BMC Public Health*. 14 (60) [online] Available at: www.biomedcentral.com/1471-2458/14/60 (accessed 7 August 2014).

Murray, C and Newby, H (2012) Data Resource Profile: United Nations Children's Fund (UNICEF). *International Journal of Epidemiology*. 41: pp 1595–1601.

Natrass, N (2014) Millennium Development Goal 6: AIDS and the International Health Agends. *Journal of Human Development*. 15 (2–3): pp 232–246.

Nayar, K (2013) Universalizing Health Services in India: The Techno-managerial Fix. *Indian Journal of Public Health*. 57 (4): pp 248–253.

Penn, H (2005) *Unequal Childhoods. Young Children's Lives in Poor Countries*. London: Routledge.

Schäferhoff, M, Schrade, C and Yamey, G (2010) Financing Maternal and Child Health – What Are the Limitations in Estimating Donor Flows and Resource Needs? *PLoS Med*. 7 (7) [online] Available at: www.plosmedicine.org (accessed 6 August 2014).

Sen, G and Mukherjee, A (2014) No Empowerment without Rights, No Rights without Politics: Gender-Equality, MDGs and the Post 2015 Development Agenda. *Journal of Human Development and Capabilities*. 15 (2–3): pp 188–202.

Stuckler, D, Basyu, S and McKee, M (2010) Drivers of Inequality in Millennium Development Goal Progress: A Statistical Analysis. *PLoS Med*. 7 (3) [online] Available at: www.plosmedicine.org (accessed 6 August 2014).

United Nations (2000) 55/2 United Nations Millennium Declaration. [online] Available at: www.un.org/millennium/declaration/ares552e.htm (accessed 7 August 2014).

United Nations (2014a) Millennium Summit (6–8 September 2000). [online] Available at: www.un.org/en/events/pastevents/millennium_summit.shtml (accessed 7 August 2014).

United Nations (2014b) *Open Working Group proposal for Sustainable Development Goals*. [online] available at: https://sustainabledevelopment.un.org (accessed 26 February 2015)

UNICEF (2004) *UNICEF'S Strengths and Weaknesses: A Summary of Key Internal and External Institutional Reviews and Evaluations Conducted from 1992–2004*. New York: UNICEF.

UNICEF (2013) UNICEF's Vision. [online] Available at: www.unicef.org/parmo/files/UNICEF_Mission.pdf (accessed 4 August 2014).

UNICEF (2014) *The State of the World's Children in Numbers. Every Child Counts: Revealing Disparities, Advancing Children's Rights*. New York: UNICEF.

WHO (1946) *Preamble to the Constitution of the World Health Organization as Adopted by the International Health Conference*. New York: Official Records of the World Health Organization.

WHO (2013) Mental Health: A State of Well-Being. [online] Available at: www.who.int/features/factfiles/mental_health/en/ (accessed 3 August 2014).

Woods, N (2006) *The Globalizers: The IMF, the World Bank, and Their Borrowers*. New York: Cornell University Press.

World Bank (2014) Mission. [online] Available at: www.worldbank.org/en/about (accessed 5 August 2014).

World Bank (2014a) International Development Association Voting Power of Executive Directors. [online] Available at: http://siteresources.worldbank.org/BODINT/Resources/278027-1215524804501/IDAEDsVotingTable.pdf (accessed 6 August 2014).

7 Global inequalities and children

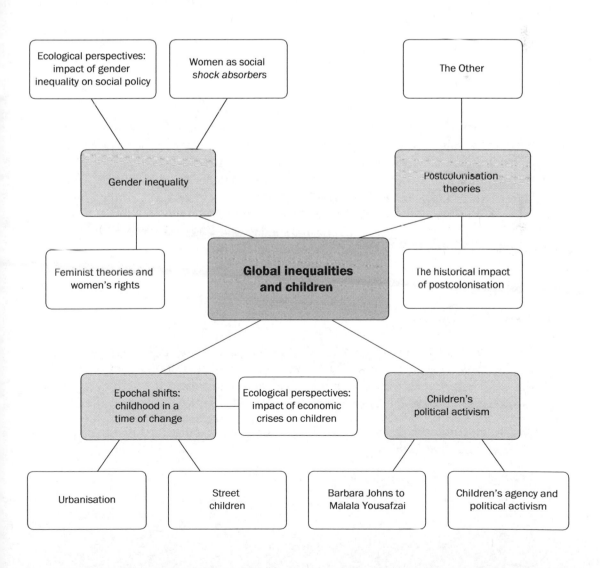

Ecological perspectives: impact of gender inequality on social policy

Women as social *shock absorbers*

The Other

Gender inequality

Postcolonisation theories

Feminist theories and women's rights

Global inequalities and children

The historical impact of postcolonisation

Epochal shifts: childhood in a time of change

Ecological perspectives: impact of economic crises on children

Children's political activism

Urbanisation

Street children

Barbara Johns to Malala Yousafzai

Children's agency and political activism

If men are unable to perceive critically the themes of their time, and thus to intervene actively in reality, they are carried along in the wake of change. They see that the times are changing, but are submerged in that change and so cannot discern its dramatic significance.

(Freire, 1969, p 7)

Introduction

An increasingly important area for discussion in the realm of global childhood studies is the way inequalities between and within nations impact children. This chapter is divided into four parts.

1. Postcolonisation theories will support an analysis of how the history of colonialism shapes the experiences of inequality in the lives of children.

2. Epochal shifts analyses childrens' experiences resulting from the current global economic uncertainty.

3. Gender inequalities examines how this impacts upon the lives of children and families.

4. Finally, children's agency through political activism when facing inequality analyses how children face the challenges inequality brings to their lives.

Inequality matters. It matters when it is about access to resources, income and freedoms of expression. Inequality is about opportunities and outcomes (OECD, 2008). The quote at the start of this chapter is by one of twentieth century's most influential educationalist, Paulo Freire. Freire highlights a concern about how ordinary people, living in a world undergoing radical change, risk being lost and marginalised by those seeking power through oppression and control. For Freire, the future lay in education that would create dialogues and respect between people in order to overcome social injustice and inequality. While his ideas have been critiqued and arguably subdued in recent times (see McLaren and Leonard, 2004), 45 years later Freire's concerns remain pertinent to the world many children experience today.

Critical questions

In his iconic work, Pedagogy of the Oppressed *(see Freire, 2006, with an insightful introduction by Donaldo Macedo), Freire argues that education is not a neutral tool but a system that can work to create conformity with authority, or to bring freedom through developing skills of criticality and creativity.*

Within your practice reflect upon the system of education you are engaged in with children and their families.

» *In what ways does it work to develop conformity?*

» *In what way does it work to develop creativity and criticality?*

» *Now apply the same analysis to your current studies. How does engaging in undergraduate or graduate studies work towards your freedom and/or conformity?*

» *What meaning can you draw from your conclusions to develop your practice and your studies?*

This chapter explores how global systems of inequality impact upon the lives of children and their families. When Freire sought to change the lives of people who had experienced generations of oppression he was reflecting upon the impact of centuries of colonialist rule within his native Brazil. Freire introduces early postcolonisation theories through his writing.

Postcolonisation theories

Postcolonisation theories encompasses a range of critical theories from ethnography, postmodernism, Marxism and feminism. This chapter considers the role postcolonisation theories have on creating inequalities that impact the lives of children across the world. Note that it does not refer to one postcolonisation theory because, much like feminist theories, there is no one definable theory to be applied but rather a collection of ideas and critiques that seek to challenge inequality globally.

Paul Young presents a series of interesting questions that are helpful if you are approaching postcolonisation theories for the first time.

> *Do you feel that your own people and country are somehow always positioned outside the mainstream? Have you ever felt that the moment you said the word 'I', that 'I' was someone else, not you? That in some obscure way, you were not the subject of your own sentence? Do you ever feel that whenever you speak, you have already in some sense been spoken for? Or that when you hear others speaking, that you are only ever going to be the object of that speech? Do you sense that those speaking would never think of trying to find out how things seem to you, from where you are? That you live in a world of others, a world that exists for others?'*
>
> (Young, 2003, p 1)

It is these kinds of questions that led to the development of postcolonisation theories. These theories relate to the impact of 400 years of colonisation both on those who colonised and on those who were colonised and they question and challenge the continuing dominant Western view of the world. They challenge a view of the world that causes global divisions we recognise in terms such as *North and South, East and West, First and Third World, the developed and developing nations.* This chapter explores how that legacy of colonisation continues to impact the lives of children and families today.

The historical impact of postcolonisation

Colonial rule by and through European nations resulted in nine-tenths of the world's land mass coming under the control of those European powers by the nineteenth century. Control of the native peoples in these countries was managed by a system of hegemonic policies that served to legitimise Western control through subjugation. Policies that sought to *divide and conquer* meant that creating tensions between ethnic groups served to better control colonised peoples through disempowerment. The imposition of Western languages, religion, political and economic processes positioned those under colonial rule as *uncivilised, child-like, feminine* and in need of saving. In addition, the legacy of slavery created divisions along lines of race and class, still seen in nations today from the United States to Brazil.

Following the Second World War, the mid- to late twentieth century saw the move for independence (see MacQueen, 2007) and the transition of these newly created nations from colonialism to postcolonialism. The divisions and impositions of Western systems of government have made these transitions at times terrible and bloody (as seen in the conflicts in Rwanda and DRC).Yet gaining independence and the creation of nation-states that emerge from divided ethnic groups has demonstrated the achievements of which people are capable.

Postcolonisation theories challenge how the people of nations once subject to colonial rule are now in positions of inequality compared with the nations that once controlled them. This is evident on the macro level through economic trading systems imposed by colonial nations and which left newly independent nations at a disadvantage. At the meso level, Western political systems of democracy had to be managed within newly independent nations comprised of peoples who for centuries under colonial rule were divided into elitist and under-class ethnic groups. At the micro level postcolonisation theories consider how individuals and communities seek to define their cultural identity as separate from that of dominant Western cultural ideas. Postcolonisation also reflects much of the approaches taken to once colonised nations that have become the recipient of aid provision (see Penn, 2005, for a comprehensive critique of the aid provision).

The Other

Postcolonisation theories also have much to say about the construction of the *Other* and *Otherness*. This concept, first proposed by Emmanuel Levinas, has been applied to post-colonial studies (see Said, 1978). Otherness positions us as the known and understood against the Other who is unknown and cannot be understood in our terms. Essentially the Other can be harmed and their identity lost by those who seek to *grasp* at understanding and defining, and in so doing seek to make the Other the same. Done well, postcolonial theories do not seek to define the unknown (Other) as a victim or exotic. Rather they offer a way to recognise difference that allows the voices of those who have been oppressed to be heard.

As an example consider the current discussions around women and girls wearing the niqab (the cloth covering the face worn by some Muslim women in public). This is a complex issue that combines diverse ideas about the role of gender, culture, politics and religion within multicultural communities.

Critical questions

Return to the questions posed in the quote from Robert Young at the start of this section. Spend some time researching the issues around the debates in France, Belgium and the United Kingdom.

»   *How has the current debate on wearing of the niqab positioned the Muslim community as Other?*

»   *What view of the Muslim woman has been created as a result of these controversies within these societies?*

»   *How do laws which force women to wear the niqab sit against laws which force women not to wear it?*

»   *How do you think these discourses impact on the experiences of children growing up within these communities?*

The impact postcolonisation theories have on children forms part of the contemporary discourses of childhood that see childhood as multiple and ever changing. MacNaughton (2005) presents an account of how the Australian colonial history speaks to the postcolonial Othering of those who are not of white, European descent. In Australian society postcolonial theories have a resonance on the Othering of children from non-European groups within society. The study below reflects this.

CASE STUDY

Yeo, S (2003) Bonding and Attachment of Australian Aboriginal Children. Child Abuse Review. *12: pp 292–304.*

In her study Yeo explored how assessments made by case workers about the bonding and attachment of Aboriginal children, when deciding if they should be removed into care, might reflect ethnocentric views of attachment. The study reports that in 2003, Aboriginal children were nine times more likely than other children to be removed from their homes. Yeo raises the importance of recognising cultural differences when making these assessments. She analyses the core hypotheses of attachment, namely:

*   caregiver sensitivity to the child's needs;

*   provision of a secure base from which children explore; and

*   that attachment results in socially competent adults.

She concludes that cultural differences that exist between Aboriginal and European parenting strategies trouble any attempt at making a direct comparison about what secure attachment between the two cultures should look like.

She found that Aboriginal infants, unlike European Australian children, had multiple caregivers with close kinship bonds that went beyond the nuclear family; children were often not weaned off breast feeding until three to five years of age. In line with many other collectivist societies, Aboriginal children were not encouraged to explore their world prior to two years of age or to focus sociability beyond the group carers, and they were discouraged from expressing negative emotions to adults. Finally, definitions of what constituted a socially competent adult did not match Western ideas of autonomy and assertiveness, instead favouring commitment and support to the community. While Yeo's research with Aboriginal communities cannot generalise caregiving to all Aboriginal families it does reflect the cultural nature of attachment and its significance when this is used to make judgements about caregiving.

The study demonstrates the way both the colonised and the coloniser become intertwined. Within Australian society the two communities live with the legacy of colonisation that impacts on the experiences of children today. That legacy is also lived within contemporary British society, and postcolonisation theories have much to support analysis of the care and education provision for all children within this society.

Critical questions

Reflect upon the discourses of attachment you see with children and their families within your practice.

»   *Taking the ideas of postcolonisation theories and the idea of the Other, what evidence do you see that the perspectives of diverse cultures are seen within your setting?*

»   *What does your setting teach children about race and difference that is meaningful and moves beyond a* tourist curriculum *approach?*

Postcolonial theories have much to say about the positioning of children in an international perspective. Cannella and Viruru (2004) analyse how Western, scientific studies have helped to create an idea of children and childhood that supports a notion of universal characteristics (see Chapter 1). Throughout this chapter analysis of the experience of children will gain a depth if the principles of postcolonisation theories are engaged with. The essential elements that consider the impact of power discourses between unequal groups have much to learn from postcolonial theories.

Epochal shifts: childhood in a time of change

Ecological perspectives: impact of economic crises on children

The closing months of 2008 heralded a time of economic crises not seen since the Great Depression of the 1930s. The collapse of financial institutes in the United States and Europe have heralded a time of real economic difficulties in global markets across the world. Reductions in the European and American economies have led to a contagion of global economic uncertainty, and rising fuel and food prices that continue to impact upon those already living on the global economic margins. Inequalities of wealth become even more visible in such times. A report by UNICEF (Mendoza and Strand, 2009) identified that, at a macro level, developing nations were the ones most likely to suffer from the economic crises

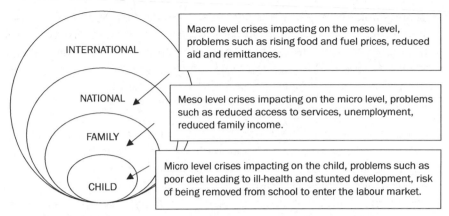

Figure 7.1 *An ecological perspective of how economic crises impact upon children*

with problems such as decreased trade and reduced expenditure by wealthier nations on aid budgets. Applying an ecological perspective reveals how problems in the macro level global economy are transferred down to the micro level, with the poorest families experiencing the full impact. For children living in families who lack the resources to buffer themselves from economic hardship, the economic crisis becomes a tangible reality (see Figure 7.1). Furthermore, for children the lack of nutrients can lead to poor physical and cognitive development, which, combined with reduced access to education, increases the risk of diminished life chances as they enter adulthood. Contemporary financial problems not only impact the current generation but are likely to influence future generations as these children grow and become adults with children to support.

Urbanisation

The downturn in the global economic crises comes at a time of increased urbanisation in developing countries. The rise in people living in urban areas, arguably, brings new possibilities for development. The centralising of resources and services, if managed well, can bring advantages over services that are scattered across rural communities. In addition, urbanisation offers opportunities for social mobility and empowerment, particularly for women (Martine, 2007).

However, the rise in urbanisation does not follow a universal pattern and within nations presents different challenges. Urbanisation is not always a movement into large, well-established cities; smaller cities and large towns also experience influx from the rural areas. Such urban environments may be less able to cope, while the triggers that compel the move are diverse. In sub-Saharan Africa, for example, small cities and the movement of people into them are often linked to war or famine and are compounded by the prevalence of HIV/AIDS. India, despite emerging as one of the fast growing economies, continues to comprise a substantial rural population and has to cope with the challenges of creating transport links across such a large country.

An inequality of wealth and opportunity within these expanding urban areas has become a growing concern. While rural poverty continues to be higher than urban poverty, the *Global*

Monitoring Report (World Bank, 2013) puts the estimate for the global number living in urban slums at 1 billion, with many of the urban poor living in large towns. A lack of proper urban planning can result in poor sanitation and access to health services, while insecurity about legal rights to land means that those who raise complaints risk eviction and harassment.

Street children

For children, the increase in urbanisation and the challenge of inequalities of resources and wealth within cities has led to the phenomena of *street children*. Street children have become a growing focus of research and media attention since the 1970s. In 2011 the UN Resolution on Street Children was drawn up by the UN Human Rights Council. Within the resolution there is recognition that street children are a global phenomena that need further research (see Chapter 8) and that there is a gender aspect to children's experiences. One of the problems of policies and studies of street children surrounds the lack of a clear definition. General definitions focus on the children's relationship with the urban environment, the *streets* in the wider sense and the lack of adequate parental supervision. Thomas De Benitez (2011) highlights that attempts to define street children have progressed from simple categorisation of children who either live on the street (*street living children*) or spend the day working on the streets and return home at night (*street working children*) to a contemporary, socially constructed view that street children are not a homogenous group but rather children who are often viewed by wider society to be *out of place* (see Ennew and Swart-Kruger, 2003) but who can be considered through their relationships with their environment. This, more complex view, sees children as agents who construct their own childhoods within the social environments they inhabit. From this perspective street children can be viewed less as voiceless victims or delinquents to be managed but more as active participants in a rights agenda.

CASE STUDY

Grugel, J and Ferreira, F (2012) Street Working Children, Children's Agency and the Challenge of Children's Rights: Evidence from Minas Gerais, Brazil. Journal of International Development. *24: pp 828–840.*

There has been a history of social debate in Brazil over child labour and child rights since the country ratified the United Nations Convention on the Rights of the Child (UNCRC). Bolsa Familia is an intervention programme implemented by the current government of Brazil aimed at reducing child poverty. One intervention is the conditional cash transfer given to low income households who send their children to school. This has been generally agreed to be successful. As per the policy, cash incentives are given to parents not to send their children to work but to school instead; this should result in a decline in the numbers of children working on the streets of Brazil's cities. However, policies aimed at rewarding parents for not sending children out to work have both limitations and unintended consequences. It can be argued that this approach does not recognise the children; it fails to consider the complexity of reasons why children work on the streets and their agency. In this study researchers surveyed over 3000 children in 2007 working on the streets of cities in Minas Gerais, Brazil's second largest state. Their main findings were that:

- 17 per cent of street workers were girls;

- 70 per cent were over 10 years old;

- 80 per cent said they slept in their parents' or close relatives' house;

- almost 20 per cent had no significant family ties;

- children had clear stratified work activities depending on the age and gender;

- jobs more likely to be rewarded with generous tips were dominated by boys;

- girls who worked were more likely to be involved in selling goods and some in prostitution;

- only a small number (less than 5 per cent) worked because their parents made them;

- less than 2 per cent reported that they were working because they had dropped out of school;

- 90 per cent of 10-year-olds said they went to school full time;

- more than 80 per cent of 12-year-olds said they were attending school – this fell after 12 years of age;

- 35 per cent reported giving their earnings to their parents;

- more than 30 per cent reported spending their earnings on themselves;

- girls were more likely than boys to give their earnings to their family;

- 70.4 per cent of children aged between 10 and 14 years said they '*liked*' or '*liked a lot*' working on the streets;

- children reported reasons why they liked working on the streets as:

  - being away from home;

  - avoiding unpaid work;

  - escaping violence at home;

  - the sociability of the street;

  - the absence of adult supervision;

  - watching television through shop windows.

The researchers concluded that social welfare programmes, although they had reduced the poverty of families, had not resulted in an end to poor children working on the streets for money. These children appeared to combine work with some degree of school attendance which suggests that the lives of street children are more complex, especially when considered in terms of the children's rights agenda.

Critical questions

» *Using the various approaches to defining street children, analyse the case study. Consider how your analysis alters when these children are viewed as:*

   – *antisocial, to be feared and managed;*

   – *victims, to be protected through welfare provision;*

   – *active participants, to be listened to.*

» *What are the benefits and challenges to these different approaches?*

» *How do the ideas of Paulo Freire inform this discussion of managing poverty and social inequality?*

» *What does this case study tell us about the way macro level policies can impact upon micro level experiences?*

Gender inequality

The greatest inequality which currently exists globally is the inequality between men and women. Gender inequality is evident across all nations, both rich and poor. It is through gender inequality that the utmost loss in the potential of all humans is felt. A report to the United Nations in 2009 on emerging issues of gender in the financial crises highlighted that it is women from poor communities who bear the greatest burden; as unemployment rises it is women who are most likely to be in poorly paid, less secure work; work which frequently requires them to spend longer hours away from their children. This will often result in girls being removed from school in order to care for younger siblings. In addition, rising ill-health through reduced access to medical support has resulted in increased care loads within families, loads which female members of the family are the most likely to meet.

Women as social *shock absorbers*

Esprey et al (2010) state that women will often act as *shock absorbers* in poor families; this can mean, for example, women reducing their own dietary intake when food is short and it is women who are most likely to become the object of increased domestic violence. As a recent study on women's access to justice in Vietnam reports (UNODC, 2013), social views that are tolerant of domestic violence against women (VAW) mean that those who experience domestic violence within the home (an estimated 58 per cent of women in Vietnam) face enormous difficulties in accessing justice despite changes made to the country's laws. This highlights the fact that enshrining equality in legislation or policies is not the end of the problem; the difference between de jure and de facto gender equality remains an issue not only in Vietnam.

Critical questions

Consider the girls in Brazil who engaged with Grugel and Ferreira's study.

» *How do their experiences of street working differ to those of the boys?*

» In what ways do these girls' experiences reflect broader gender inequalities within the society as highlighted in the UN reports above?

Ecological perspective: impact of gender inequality on social policy

National policies, such as Balsa Familia, seek to support children in poor families at times of economic hardship. However, these are not always equitable when analysed against how they might seek to address gender inequalities. For example, public works programmes aimed at using funding to engage workers from poor communities in paid work projects are often unsuitable for women or lack the flexibility that women's care requirements demand. Holmes and Jones (2009) argue that gender inequality needs to be addressed from the macro to the micro level if it is to have a meaningful impact upon the experiences of women and children (see Figure 7.2). In terms of the benefits to children, gender equality matters. The children of women who have little or no education living in impoverished communities are particularly vulnerable. In addition, these women have reduced access to higher paid, skilled employment and managerial roles. At a macro level, less women involved in decision-making capacities in government often means that the needs of women are not given due consideration in both project planning and policy-making.

	RISKS	POLICIES AND LEGISLATION	RELATED GENDER ISSUES
Macro level	• Rising food and fuel prices. • Reduced aid and remittances. • Violence against women (VAW).	Policies on: • Investment into services such as health and education. • Investment in infrastructure programmes such as transport. Legislation on VAW.	• Lack of gender integration when making legislation and policy choices, planning and analysis. • Recognising that gender inequality is part of social exclusion.
Meso level	• Reduced access to services such as health and education. • Unemployment. • Reduced family income. • Difficulties accessing legal rights.	• Governance of policies at a local level. • Effective delivery of policies. • Effective implementation and monitoring of laws.	• Engendering the translation and implementation process of policy at this level. • Gendered hierarchy practices that value the employment of men over women.
Micro level	• Poor diet leading to ill-health and stunted development. • Risk of being removed from school to enter the labour market or for carer roles.	• Families' capacity to sustain an income/livelihood. • Families' capacity to provide food and security. • Gender roles and female subordination within families.	• Gender and generational roles and power relations within families. • Societal views on domestic VAW.

Figure 7.2 The way gender inequalities impact upon social policies from macro to micro level

If gender inequality is to be addressed, decisions need to be made at the macro level; as Fildis (2011) argues, policy-making aimed at addressing the impact of the economic crises as well as other long-term poverty management policies needs to embed the well-being of women into the process. Policies should reflect the need for gender equality in terms of women's access to education and financial credit and to ensure that public projects provide economic opportunities for women. Gaining access to financial credit enables women to set up business, which allows increased engagement for them in the society. Indeed the importance placed on gender equality in broader social development is reflected in the decisions being planned for the post-2015 Millennium Development Goals (MDGs) (see Chapter 6).

Critical questions

Spend some time using the online resources available from the United Nations, UNICEF and UN Women to research how policies and programmes for the post-2015 MDGs approach gender equality.

Consider the following.

» *How are decisions being made at this macro level likely to address meso level social and political views that will enable women fair access to provision?*

» *How does the rhetoric being presented by these organisations position women? How is gender equality linked to other goals being reached? How often are women described purely as individuals with rights?*

An ecological perspective leads us to face the fact that gender inequality is a problem that cannot be seen purely in economic terms, it spans cultural, social and political domains. There are limited gains in educating girls if they are then denied access to employment or opportunities to contribute to society. As the OECD report 'Closing the Gap' (OECD, 2012) identifies, addressing gender inequality means ensuring gender equality in macro and meso level policy-making, education, employment and access to entrepreneurship.

Feminist theories and women's rights

It is worth pausing to consider some of the use that has been made by the application of feminist theory in developing a contemporary understanding of international approaches to addressing gender inequality. Prior to the women's rights movements of the 1970s, women tended to be viewed, from a Western perspective, in terms of mothers and wives. Western institutions sought to address gender inequality through improving men's economic prospects, a *trickle down* approach which would therefore benefit wives and daughters. In the 1970s gender equality became a rights-based issue that aimed to overcome inequality by giving women access to the economic prospects through a top-down provision of aid that would empower women to overcome inequalities. However, this failed to address the problems women and their children faced as it viewed women as a homogenous group, and poorly directed financing did little to improve the position of women within their societies. From the 1980s a shift in the way gender equality is positioned in terms of the provision of aid to families has sought to empower women through aid provision that crosses a number of the needs of women and young children through health, education and political identity that takes a bottom-up approach (Taylor, 2009). However, the reality of implementing such changes is recognised as having limited benefits unless entrenched inequalities within broad social, political and economic institutions are addressed; this will be the challenge that faces global policies post-2015.

If the debate surrounding gender equality is to progress then the impact of gender inequality on children becomes imperative. If gender inequality can only be addressed through challenging deeply entrenched views on the role of women, then children play an integral role in this. On the micro level, the role of the family as a gendered space in the lives of children has been discussed in Chapter 3.

The discussion of gender inequality leads us to return to the role of children's agency and the impact children can have on addressing the inequalities they are faced with.

Children's political activism

Children's agency and political activism

This chapter has considered that for many children inequalities across all strata of their lives mean that their childhoods cannot be seen in terms of innocence and protection. As has already been discussed, children are often distanced from the decisions being made that impact upon their lives (see Chapter 1, children's agency; and Chapter 5, children's rights agenda). It is now important to consider the role of children's agency demonstrated through their engagement in political activism. Certainly, children's engagement in political activism shows a lineage of their impact in actively fighting inequality from Barbara Johns in 1951 to the Soweta uprisings in 1976. Wells (2009) lists four characteristics of children's engagement in political activism:

1. most are older teenagers;
2. the school often forms the focus of political mobilisation;
3. it is not merely about intergenerational conflict.
4. unless it forms part of a state-wide revolution, children's political activism is pursued by the minority.

Digital technology, globalisation and the growth of social media arguably suggest a further characteristic that these spaces influence and are utilised by children engaging in international political and social activism.

It is worth noting that when children's agency is exhibited in terms of political activism, Wells (2009) also points out that the term *child* is often supplanted by the word *youth*. While this reflects the view that children who engage in political activism are likely to be older teenagers, arguably it also places them outside the *norm* of childhood. These children challenge the dyadic roles of the child as decision-recipient and the adult as decision-maker; the term *youth* serves to set them outside these roles. In fact, in a political context, children can be seen as citizens who are part of a community while also being seen as incapable of being full citizens because of their lack of rational thought. This is evident within current debates on when children can be considered old enough to vote. Certainly, from an ecological basis, the way societies engage or ignore children within their political debates is likely to determine the type of political adults they become.

From Barbara Johns to Malala Yousafzai

The term *youth* also implies *male* and returns us to the issue of gender inequality. The story of Malala Yousafzai, the Pakistani schoolgirl shot by the Taliban, not only brings the history of children's political activism into contemporary discourses of childhood but challenges any gender bias. The political uprising that she has triggered, both within Pakistan and internationally, reflects the impact that children's involvement in politics can have. The micro level actions of these children can have macro level repercussions in the political discourses that underlie inequality. The story of Malala continues to unfold alongside the debate Pakistan and other countries are having on the role Western nations play in the politics of their region (Fazl-E-Haider, 2013). Yet in this discussion it is important to warn against seeing children as *political saviours* (Wells, 2009, p 139). Children are as capable of acts of political terror as they are of political reform. The role of children within the Hitler Youth and the Red Guard highlights this reality.

Critical questions

It is worth gaining a broader historical understanding of children's political activism by researching the history of child political activism. Exploring the lives and experiences of Barbara Johns, Tsietsi Mashinini and Malala Yousafzai in addition to the role of children in national revolutions such as the Red Guard in China's Cultural Revolution of the 1960s, consider the following.

»   *How does the legacy of colonisation influence the inequalities these children faced?*

»   *What do their experiences tell you about the position of the Other within their society?*

Beyond these key figures who stand out within the discourse of children's political activism there exist numerous others who engage in fighting inequalities within their own communities. Bosco (2010) helps with this discussion by posing the question '*what defines political acts?*' Certainly the acts seen through researching the histories of children such as Barbara Johns and Tsietsi Mashinini can include high-risk acts in the face of inequality. However, Bosco's (2010) study of local activism among Mexican communities in a poor immigrant district of San Diegio, California, demonstrated not only smaller, micro level acts of children's political activism but also the way young children engaged in local activism. Bosco (2010) reports that young children participated in local advocacy through acts such as translating for their mothers and engaging in *playful* activism such as car washes, neighbourhood clean-ups and community service projects. These more subtle acts of political activism by children reflect the breadth of engagement children demonstrate.

While children's engagement in political activism can be seen as a way of addressing inequalities within their communities it also offers the opportunity for children to challenge the way they are frequently presented.

CASE STUDY

Sircar, O and Dutta, D (2011) Beyond Compassion: Children of Sex Workers in Kolkata's Sonagachi. Childhood. 18 (3): pp 333–349.

In March 2009, 3000 children as young as six years old, the sons and daughters of sex workers from Kolkata's Songachi region of India, marched through the streets demanding their mothers' rights to a livelihood and their right to freedom from stigma and discrimination. The children were all members of a collective they had started called *Amra Padatik* (We are Foot Soldiers). The researchers interviewed children from the collective and what emerged was not the passive victims they were frequently portrayed as, but rather active agents engaged in political activism to demand rights for themselves and their mothers. The children's relationship with their mothers was more complicated than often presented in the media which tended to present the mothers as abusive or neglectful of their children. In the study the children have used the collective to tackle a range of issues from unscrupulous landlords to challenging government policy to criminalise their mothers' clients. In addition, the children have engaged in wider political activism, creating political posters on Israeli bombing of Lebanon.

The resilience the children showed challenges the traditional *compassion-driven* response of *raid, rescue and rehabilitation* when faced with the hardships of their lives. The study proposes that rather than a universal compassion of idealized childhoods that result in the forced removal of the children from their mothers, a counter-response of resilience, reworking and resistance is possible. Through the collective, the children highlighted their lack of rights, reduced educational opportunities and social stigmatisation. The researchers conclude that a more meaningful response to the children would be recognition and support for the *resilience, reworking and resistance* they demonstrated. They argue that focusing on the opinions of the children central to the issue would support a more meaningful response.

The children in this study, much like the street children discussed in the earlier case study, demonstrate agency in addressing challenges within their lives.

Critical questions

» *What does the case study tell you about the way children's political activism can challenge the way they are perceived within their community and wider society?*

» *Return to the questions asked of the earlier case study – how does your analysis alter when these children are viewed as:*

- *antisocial, to be feared and managed;*

- *victims, to be protected through welfare provision;*

- *active participants, to be listened to.*

» *Analyse the way the children in this case study have chosen to engage in political activism while the children working on the streets of Minas Gerais have not.*

» *Why do you think the children show different approaches to their situations?*

» *What does this add to the discourse of diverse and multiple childhoods?*

Critical reflections

This chapter has examined inequalities both within and between nations and the way they impact children. The consideration of postcolonial theories helps to place a historical perspective upon contemporary issues and to inform analysis of the way Western views of children and childhood permeate international studies and organisations. Having read this chapter you should now be able to understand how to apply postcolonial theories and the ecological systems theories to your analysis of the way inequalities shape childhood. In addition to using this chapter to support your study of inequality, use the discussions here as a starting point to reflect upon, and inform, your own practice when working with families and children.

References

Bosco, F (2010) Play, Work or Activism? Broadening the Connection between Political and Children's Geographies. *Children's Geographies*. 8 (4): pp 381–390.

Cannella, G and Viruru, R (2004) *Childhood and Postcolonization: Power, Education and Contemporary Practice*. London: Routledge.

Ennew, J and Swart-Kruger, J (2003) Introduction: Homes, Places and Spaces in the Construction of Street Children and Street Youth. *Children, Youth and Environments*. 13(1): pp 81–104.

Espey, J, Harper, C and Jones, N (2010) Crisis, Care and Childhood: The Impact of Economic Crisis on Care Work in Poor Households in the Developing World. *Gender and Development*. 18 (2): pp 291–307.

Fazl-E-Haider, S (2013) Malala versus Extremism. *Harvard International Review*. Spring: pp 73–76.

Fildis, A T (2011) The Welfare of Women and Children during the Global Economic Crisis. *Trakya Universitesi Sosyal Bilimler Dergisi*. 13 (2): pp 297–308.

Freire, P (1969) *Education: The Practice of Freedom*. Translated by M Bergman Ramos, 1974. London: Writers and Readers Publishing Cooperative.

Freire, P (2006) *Pedagogy Of The Oppressed. Thirtieth Anniversary Edition*. Translated by M Bergman Ramos, 1970. New York: Continuum International Publishing.

Grugel, J and Ferreira, F (2012) Street Working Children, Children's Agency and the Challenge of Children's Rights: Evidence from Minas Gerais, Brazil. *Journal of International Development*. 24: pp 828–840.

MacNaughton, G (2005) *Doing Foucault in Early Childhood Studies*. London: Routledge.

MacQueen, N (2007) *Colonialism*. Harlow: Pearson Education Limited.

Martine, G (2007) *State of World Population 2007: Unleashing the Potential of Urban Growth*. London: United Nations Population Fund.

Mclaren, P. and Leonard, P. (eds) (2004) *Paulo Freire: A Critical Encounter*. London: Routledge.

Menoza, R and Strand, E (2009) *Social and Economic Policy Working Brief: How Economic Shocks Affect Poor Households and Children*. UNICEF Policy and Practice. [online] Available at: www.unicef.org/eapro/ESPWB_July_2009_How_Economic_Shocks_Affect_Children.pdf (accessed 12 October 2013).

OECD (2008) *Growing Unequal? Income Distribution and Poverty in OECD Countries*. OECD Publishing.

OECD (2012) *Closing the Gender Gap: Act Now*. OECD Publishing.

Penn, H (2005) *Unequal Childhoods. Young Children's Lives in Poor Countries*. London: Routledge.

Said, E (1978) *Orientalism. Western Concepts of the Orient*. London: Penguin Books.

Sircar, O and Dutta, D (2011) Beyond Compassion: Children of Sex Workers in Kolkata's Sonagachi. *Childhood*. 18 (3): pp 333–349.

Taylor, M (2009) Gender and Development, in McCann, G and McCloskey, S (eds) *From the Local to the Global: Key Issues in Development Studies,* 2nd edn. London: Pluto Press.

The World Bank (2013) *Global Monitoring Report 2013: Rural-Urban Dynamics and the Millennium Development Goals*. The World Bank / The International Monetary Fund. [online] Available at: http://go.worldbank.org/60UGFNSODO (accessed 13 October 2014).

Thomas De Benitez, S (2011) *State of the world's Street Children: Research*. London: Consortium For Street Children.

United Nations (2009) Emerging Issues: The Gender Perspectives of the Financial Crises. Commission on the Status of Women. Fifty-Third Session, New York, 2–13 March 2009 Interactive Expert Panel.

UNICEF (2013) *Syria Crises. Bi-weekly Humanitarian Situation Report*. [online] Available at: www.unicef.org/appeals/syrianrefugees_sitreps.html [accessed 8 October 2013].

UNODC (2013) *Assessment of the Situation of Women in the Criminal Justice System in Viet Nam*. Hanoi.

Wells, K (2009) *Childhood in a Global Perspective*. Cambridge: Polity.

Yeo, S (2003) Boning and Attachment of Australian Aboriginal Children. *Child Abuse Review*. 12: pp 292–304.

Young, P (2003) *Postcolonialism: A Very Short Introduction*. New York: Oxford University Press.

8 Global research and the construction of childhoods

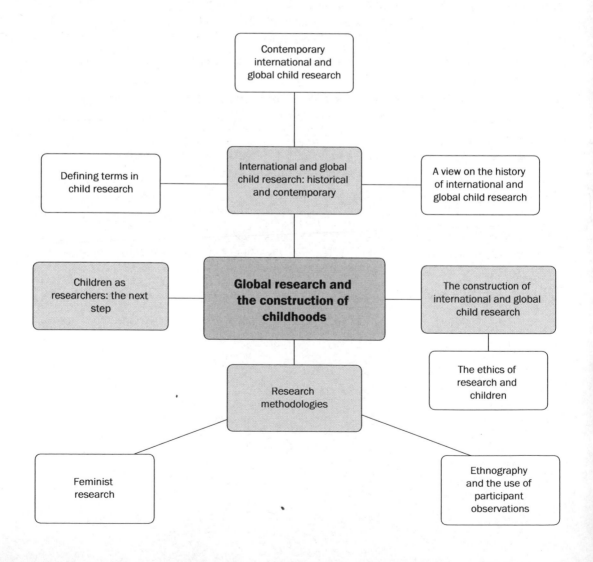

International child research does not necessarily imply a homogenized perspective, but rather a wide variety of dialogues, exchanges, debates, collaborations and reconceptualizations.

(Editorial, 1997, p 149)

Introduction

This chapter examines the role of international child research in constructing childhoods. Throughout the twentieth and twenty-first centuries international research on children and childhoods has expanded, particularly with the emergence of communication technology making possible longitudinal, macro level studies that examine childhoods across nations. As the quote above suggests, research offers the opportunity to understand children's multiple and diverse experiences of childhood in ways that are more relevant and meaningful. The role research plays in this varies from the *big* data generated in macro level transnational research to the micro level studies which *pick* at the issues impacting the lives of individual children, their families and their communities.

Yet international child research with children is not without challenges. This chapter also considers the importance of reflecting upon the validity and use made of such research and the ethical considerations concerned with how it is obtained. Research studies, particularly those conducted by governments and large international organisations such as UNICEF, frequently emphasise large issues that impact upon childhoods. This results in large studies that examine children's rights with regard to health, education, labour and exploitation across nations. Smaller studies place these issues into a local context as well as researching the details that construct children's social worlds.

Critical questions

When embarking on an examination of research it is helpful to reflect upon your own values and how they are likely to influence your approach to research. Spend some time considering the following questions on how you view the purpose of child research.

» *In your opinion, what are the purposes of child research?*

» *What ethical implications might emerge from these purposes?*

» *What roles does the researcher play in such research?*

» *How are children viewed in such research?*

Keep your answers to these questions and return to them after reading this chapter.

This chapter is divided into four parts:

1.   international and global child research: historical and contemporary;

2.   the construction of international and global child research;

3.   research methodologies;

4.   children as researchers – the next step.

International and global child research: historical and contemporary

When discussing the wider issues around child research from an international perspective it is useful to begin by defining the terms used within this chapter.

Defining terms in child research

International child research studies are conducted across one or more nations, such as research involving children or factors that influence childhood which are explored in transnational comparative studies such as 'The State of the World's Children' (UNICEF, 2014), UNICEF's annual reporting of statistical data on children (see Chapter 6 for more details). However, international child research can also be viewed in terms of the dissemination of research conducted within different nations.

Global child research studies seek to disseminate research into childhoods from across the globe. Taking the principle Bloom et al (2006) propose when defining global health research, *global child research* emphasises smaller research studies conducted by individuals and institutions which can then be shared across nations without exclusivity or rivalry. (Indeed this is the premise for the analysis and discussion of research studies from around the world used throughout the chapters of this book.)

Both international child research and global child research emphasise the collaborative approach promoted in contemporary child research. Discussions into the role of particular research methods and methodologies as well as co-operation in generating research questions within contemporary child research have led to research being shared across nations and have become an important means of understanding the multidimensional experiences of childhood today. The means by which research is disseminated has broadened with the ongoing development of electronic communication and forums such as social media.

When engaging with such research it is important that the reader analyses not only the data being presented but also broader aspects such as the study's validity and ethical stance. Accessing research from reputable sources such as peer-reviewed journals and organisations with transparent ethical guidelines is a key starting point.

Critical question

»   *What key questions should you be asking yourself in order to understand the context of your research? How does this research compare with other studies?*

Comment

Your answers to the above question might have included the following.

»   *What does this research say about children's lives in this and other contexts?*

»   *What might this research say about childhoods in the future?*

» *What conclusions can I draw from this research?*

Child research, as with all research, is influenced by certain basic premises – who conducts the research and for what purpose; who is involved in the research and who is excluded; and who the research is aimed at. Questioning these reveals much about why particular topics are studied over others and how these are approached, constructed and presented. This is true both in large and small-scale studies. It is worth, therefore, briefly examining the history of international child research.

A view on the history of international and global child research

The history of the research of children is, in many ways, entwined within the history of social and ethnographic research (research methodologies will be discussed later in this chapter). Within Western nations the interest in the child as a being separate to that of wider society was connected to the development of education through the sixteenth and seventeenth centuries (Ariès, 1962). The child as the subject of research arguably emerged from the expansion of education as a means of social reform that began in the eighteenth century with the concepts of improving children's health and welfare as a means of supporting wider social reform, a principle which continues today.

The belief that the application of scientific methods into the social world to support welfare improvements led education reformers, such as Robert Owen, in the early nineteenth century to conclude:

> ... when it was perceived that inanimate mechanism was greatly improved by being made firm and substantial; ... it was natural to conclude that the more delicate, complex, living mechanism would be equally improved by being trained to strength and activity and that it would also prove true economy to keep it neat and clean; to treat it with kindness, that its mental movements might not experience too much irritating friction.
>
> (Owen, 1991, p 6)

These early child studies were conducted not only by reformers but by teachers, physicians and lay persons and supported changes to the education of children and also led to what has become recognised as child development research (Pols, 2002). The twentieth century saw child research become *professionalised* into the hands of psychologists and medics as the scientific approach to the research of children focused increasingly upon learning and development. This included the principles of scientific testing which influenced psychological development theories as proposed by Jean Piaget (1896–1980) and social development theories as proposed by Albert Bandura et al (1961).

While these studies embedded the notion of child development, the scientific study of children concentrated on Western childhoods based in Europe and the United States. Unlike research on children in Europe and Western nations, research on non-Western childhoods is bound to the processes and beliefs of colonialism (see Chapter 7). Anthropological studies, conducted as the progression of colonisation by European nations built momentum, saw non-Western children subsumed within research studies examining the wider societies and cultures colonialists encountered. Early historical records illustrate not only the brutality of colonialism but the contempt in which colonised people were held. The same nineteenth-century scientific principles that influenced the study of children in Europe also impacted upon the ethnographic study of colonised societies. Clair (2003) recounts how Henry Morgan's study of the Iroquois in the nineteenth century used Darwin's theory of evolution to record the *development* of cultures from the *barbaric* Iroquois to the *civilised* European. The ethnocentric aspects of the assumptions he drew reflect the views Western societies and academics held of the people they encountered as the *uncivilised savage*.

In the twentieth century the impact of the two World Wars and the rise of postcolonial theories led to ethnographic studies of non-Western societies which focused more upon patterns and communications of the societies in their studies. The rise of international organisations such as UNICEF following the Second World War (see Chapter 6) saw the emergence and growth of international research on issues specifically impacting children. The large transnational quantitative studies by these organisations have been further enabled by advances in global electronic communication and data collection systems. This has led international child research to be utilised in order to highlight issues in children's lives such as access to health, education and gender equality in order to galvanise action based predominantly on children's rights. International research into children's lives has therefore become an increasingly central role for international organisations.

Ethnographic research that examines inequalities that can arise, not only within the societies being studied but also in the way research is constructed, has led to studies of children that challenge any single truth international child research generates. The micro level studies of global childhoods are influenced by the current interest in child research that reflects an idea of multiple childhoods and multiple perspectives on childhood.

Contemporary international and global child research

As the discussion on the history of global child research suggests, the approaches taken to research children have changed in line with attitudes and perspectives on the places children and childhood hold within individual nations and internationally. The rise in prominence of children's rights across the twentieth and twenty-first centuries has shaped the view of rights that include both protection and participation (see Chapter 5). This has influenced the approaches taken to child research that expand beyond research done *on* children to include research in collaboration *with* children or indeed research which is done *by* children (Yardley, 2011). These contemporary approaches to collaboration in child research shape the view of what the purpose of child research is.

A major purpose for much of the international child research conducted today arises from the requirement to demonstrate *evidence-based practice*. This has become the basis for decisions made by policy-makers both within individual states and by international organisations. The discussion of what constitutes evidence used within policies is much debated in areas such as education (Bell and Stevenson, 2006) and global health (Buse et al, 2012). While this might lead to research aimed at presenting factual data in order to shape policy decisions, the link between the two is by no means clear and certain. The decisions of policy-makers that impact upon the lives of children rarely result from a direct link based upon research evidence, rather they are the result of numerous and complex factors which may (or may not) include research findings, or indeed may use research findings in ways the original researchers had neither envisaged nor intended.

Research perspectives: ontology and epistemology

This use of international child research to inform policy-makers highlights the different perspectives which influence research in general and child research in particular. In research, these perspectives are frequently defined through the terms ontology and epistemology. It is important to tackle these terms in order to understand why certain topics are chosen for study by organisations and individual researchers (and why certain topics are not chosen); they also support an analysis of the different approaches taken to conducting a research study. Similarly, reflecting upon our own epistemological position prompts us to recognise how this influences not only the way we approach research but also our practice with children and families.

Ontology

Ontology, in terms of international child research, questions the nature and form of the world children inhabit. We are faced with questions of how we view children, childhood and children's rights for example. From a realist view the ontology of children perceives children, their rights and their childhood as objective, separate and independent of the researcher's (or practitioner's) perception of the child, his/her rights and childhood. Waring (2012) envisages this as one end of a continuum which extends to the other ontological position, a constructivist view. From this position the researcher (or practitioner) would perceive the same children, their rights and childhoods not as objective and independent but rather as part of multiple realities that are shaped by the researcher's (and practitioner's) own experiences, values and beliefs regarding, children, children's rights and childhood. (See Further Reading for a suggestion to extend this exploration with regard to human rights.) It can be argued that the ontological perspective of those commissioning and conducting research will influence the approaches taken and leads to an examination of how epistemological approaches influence research processes.

Epistemology

Epistemology questions what constitutes knowledge and how this knowledge can be found and known. From the realist view, epistemology is knowledge captured from facts that can be directly observed or measured. This knowledge is positivist, often comprising statistical data to which theories can be applied and enabling clearly defined, objective, empirical knowledge to be generated. In contrast, a constructivist position sees knowledge as constructed from indirect, subjective, shared ideas which are then interpreted through the research to create knowledge. This interpretivist knowledge is constructed from the experiences of individual participants and researchers. To help make sense of the terms and how they inform our analysis of international research, examine two different studies referred to in Chapter 5.

CASE STUDY

In Chapter 5, two very different pieces of research where considered.

The first was:

UNICEF (2013) Child Well-being in Rich Countries: A Comparative Overview. *Innocenti Report Card 11.* Florence: UNICEF Office of Research.

The second was:

Okyere, S (2012) Are Working Children's Rights and Child Labour Abolition Complementary or Opposing Realms? *International Social Work.* **56** (1): pp 80–91.

If, as Waring (2012) suggests, ontology and epistemology exist along continuums, return to those studies and use the following questions to support your analysis of the ontological perspectives and the epistemology used to generate the knowledge they report. It would be particularly advantageous to go to the original studies.

Critical questions

» *What, in your opinion, is the ontological view UNICEF demonstrates of children's well-being? Why might they have taken this stance? Justify your answer.*

» *What, in your opinion, is the ontological perspective Okyere demonstrates in his study of child labour and child rights? Why might he have taken this stance? Justify your answer.*

» *How have these ontological perspectives influenced the way each of these studies has been approached in order for the researchers to generate knowledge of children's well-being and children's rights?*

» *If UNICEF and Okyere had taken alternate ontological perspectives on these topics, how might these studies have been constructed differently?*

Any analysis of child research, both international and global, also requires consideration of how research in these contexts is constructed, managed and conducted. This forms the second part of the chapter.

The construction of international and global child research

The expansion of child research and the relative ease of accessibility means that research increasingly influences ideas about childhoods around the world. If studying children's experiences and childhoods from a global perspective is important for those working with children and young people, then examining the mechanisms by which such research is conducted is critical to this.

The ethics of research and children

The discussion on the approaches taken to the study of children and childhood has not, as yet, considered ethics, and yet ethical questions strike at the very heart of why research is conducted on, with or by children. Ultimately ethics raise important questions such as:

- what purpose does research into children and childhoods serve?

- who benefits from the research, and how does a study benefit those children directly involved?

- how are children able to influence decisions about what research is conducted into their lives?

- how are children able to question the way they are represented in studies into their lives?

- what unseen risks to children can result from research?

While any research carries an element of risk, the power imbalance existing between adult researcher and child participant highlights the important role of ethical discussions in child research. Of course contemplating the ethical considerations of international research is inevitably entangled with wider discourses around the ethics of the relationship the wealthy minority world nations have with the less wealthy majority world nations (for an insightful discussion on these issues see Helen Penn's book listed in the Further Reading). Yet the premise of the ethics of the relationship between those commissioning and conducting research studies and those who participate in the research are key.

The ethical responsibilities those conducting the research have to those who participate, Pryke et al (2003) argue, last beyond the end of the study. Indeed the *ethics of the encounter* has become strategic in shaping much global child research. This suggests that truly ethical research happens when these encounters between researcher and participant result in a co-production of knowledge that recognises both the differences and similarities between those involved in the research process. For research involving children this reflects the ethical dilemma of research which balances children's participation rights with their protection rights. The power disparities in child research heightens the ethical principles to ensure non-maleficence within research studies, placing an obligation on researchers to ensure the ethics of an encounter that benefits children directly or indirectly involved in research. However, the realities of engaging in studies frequently result in researchers facing ethical decision-making dilemmas. The development of organisations such as Ethical Research Involving Children (ERIC, 2014) that offer guidance recognises how the growth in international and global child research has led to more researchers facing such dilemmas. The following case study describes the ethical process faced by researchers engaging in a study with children in India.

CASE STUDY

Exenberger, S (2013) The Work of Interpreters in a Cultural Sensitive Environment, in Graham, A, Powell, M, Taylor, N, Anderson, D and Fitzgerald, R (eds) Ethical Research Involving Children. *Florence: UNICEF Office of Research – Innocenti.*

The ethical dilemma arose while planning culturally sensitive, subjective indicators of children's well-being from children's and caregivers' perspectives for a research study to be conducted with children living in southern India four years after the trauma of the 2004 tsunami. The study was to be conducted by Western researchers, working for a children's aid charity, with children living in remote fishing communities who hardly spoke English and whose previous experience of Western adults was limited to the postdisaster relief aid workers.

The researchers wanted to create an atmosphere to work with the children in harmonious focus group discussions with few behavioural restrictions. However, the cultural tradition of vertical collectivism placed expectations on children's behaviour with adults that emphasised non-questioning respect, obedience, duty and loyalty. This was not conducive to the environment the researchers wished to create in order for the children to respond openly and honestly. Further the adults who would act as interpreters would also have the same cultural expectations of the children's behaviour. The researchers were faced with the ethical dilemma of engaging interpreters who could act as culture brokers with the children while integrating a different approach to working with the children without losing sight of their cultural values.

The researchers recruited one male and one female interpreter who were bilingual students from the local university's social work department. The students were to interpret in same-sex focus groups and were open to following a different approach to dealing with children without losing their own cultural values. The students received two days training in the aims of the researchers and the concepts of well-being and trauma being examined and confidentiality. A written code of conduct that covered their behaviour with the children, including why the researchers wanted them to behave in certain ways, was discussed. The interpreters were asked to interpret in short units, not to ask self-initiated questions, or engage in side-conversations with the children during the focus group and to join in games and relaxation exercises. The researchers report that these measures combined with feedback sessions with the interpreters allowed a successful study to be completed.

The case study demonstrates the importance of ethical questioning when planning research studies with any children, but particularly with children who have experienced traumatic situations such as those in this study.

Critical questions

Reflect upon the case study and consider the following questions.

» *What ontological and epistemological approaches to research might these researchers be demonstrating?*

» What ethical dilemmas might arise when engaging in focus group discussions with children in this study?

» What ethical considerations would need to be given to the interpreters?

» In your opinion, how might this study have differed if it had been conducted by staff from the local university? Justify your answer.

Clearly, the complexity of engaging in research with children presents innumerable ethical dilemmas therefore researchers need to consider the broader methodological approaches that structure child research.

Research methodologies

If the ethics of child research raises questions imperative to understanding how research on international scales is conducted, it is also valuable to recognise the role research methodologies play in the research process. As the ontological and epistemological approaches researchers take to the study of children's experiences matter, so too do the methodological theories that are employed in a study. Any discussion of research methodologies will inevitably be both complex and to some degree contentious. It is useful to view methodology in terms of how a particular perspective creates studies asking interesting and relevant questions that result in answers and/or dialogues reached through clear and rigorous analysis of the data. Research methodology also allows for exploration of issues such as the balance of power within a study.

Ethnography and the use of participant observations

Ethnography, the study of peoples and cultures, emerged from early-nineteenth-century European and American anthropological research into the study of humans. Traditionally ethnography applied participant observations to the study and analysis of peoples' everyday lives. More recently, interviewing, focus groups and digital photography have become additional methods used by ethnographic researchers. At the heart, however, remains the study of how the symbolic coding and enactments people make on the micro level of society can be used to examine broader macro level systems and institutions. Of course the study into the lives of ordinary people has always been open to criticism, particularly regarding its wider relevance; however, as Herbert (2000, p 551) extols, '*Ethnography explores the tissue of everyday life to reveal the processes and meaning which undergird social action, and which enable order to be reproduced and sometimes challenged*'.

This depth of study requires ethnographers to spend considerable lengths of time both observing and interacting with individuals in the society being studied. Therefore careful reflection by researchers on their own positionality is important in order to recognise how their values, ideas, identities and emotional responses impact upon the researcher process. Positionality helps researchers manage how to balance a sense of empathy for participants while being able to interpret data. Fundamental to this is the path that must be trodden when seeking a non-ethnocentric approach (see Chapter 1) that is capable of fairly representing the experiences of participants while being cognisant to the dangers of extreme cultural relativism. Understanding responses to ethical issues will invariably play a central role in this.

This subjective interpretation of observations has been levelled as a critique to the validity of ethnographic research. Yet interpretivist research is arguably not in itself a problem as the meaning of data both quantitative and qualitative will invariably be subject to a degree of interpretation by the researcher. The issue lies more in the degree and manner of interpreting meaning from the actions and responses of people. The challenges that ethnographers face include:

- analysing the actions and responses of participants from a cultural group to which researchers do not belong;

- knowing that participants cannot represent broader cultural and social communities;

- recognising the complexity of all cultural and social groups based upon multiple experiences and identities influenced by innumerable factors such age, gender, class, race and history;

- acknowledging that the study of societies is in itself a social act which will invariably impact upon participants.

Careful planning is needed to address these challenges. Crang and Cook (2007) argue that rather than engaging a random sample it is necessary for researchers to identify those people who are most able to give the lived experiences and perspectives in order to answer the research questions being asked. In addition they suggest the need to recognise a '*point of theoretical saturation*' (Crang and Cook, 2007, p 15) when it is apparent that the range of experiences emerging from the group have been exhausted and signals either a point to commence analysis or seek the experiences of another group. The final aspect is to prepare by examining previous research within the field of study in order to be satisfied that there is a depth to the research and that the tensions and commonalities with previous research have been adequately considered. Essentially what ethnography offers is a means of researching the subjective relationships between wider macro level social, economic and political systems through micro level communities.

CASE STUDY

Return to the case study examined in Chapter 3.

Francis-Chizororo, M (2010) Growing up Without Parents: Socialisation and Gender Relations in Orphaned-Child-Headed Households in Rural Zimbabwe. Journal of Southern African Studies. *36 (3): pp 711–727.*

This ethnographic study engaged five child-headed households (CHHs) from five villages across the rural district of Mashonaland West Province, Zimbabwe, over a three-month period. It examined how CHHs reflected broader cultural ideas of family and gender roles within the Shona communities in the area.

The researcher found that hierarchy within CHHs reflected cultural generational hierarchy found in wider society. While CHHs were spaces where these cultural norms might at times be contested, culturally specific gender roles meant elder girls might not be seen as the head of the family despite fulfilling that function.

In addition elder children did not consider themselves as a mother or father for their younger siblings, instead describing their roles as providing food and giving advice as an aunt or uncle might. Francis-Chizororo concluded that CHHs characterised places for decision-making and socialisation where power structures and gendered roles from the broader patriarchal culture put pressure on boys within the CHHs to try and maintain gendered roles which often caused tensions when girls held that role.

The researcher utilised ethnographic techniques such as participant observations, in-depth interviews, informal conversations, drama, essay writing and focus groups in order to research *with* the children rather than *on* them. Francis-Chizororo (2010, p 717) describes how after spending days and nights living with the children she then interviewed the child heads, finding

> the in-depth interview approach evoked memories that caused the children (and the researcher) to cry as they narrated the deaths of their parents or their ill treatment by relatives. ... However, while the questions raised painful issues, the children were no strangers to distress, and it was perhaps an unusual and cathartic experience to have someone listen to their stories.

Critical questions

» As a result of this research, what would you recommend NGOs consider when designing support for CHHs?

» What, in your opinion, are the advantages of ethnographic studies which listen to stories of children such as those in this study?

» What, in your opinion, are the challenges that arise from listening to these stories?

Feminist research

As ethnographic research seeks to examine the lived experiences of people in order to better understand wider social and cultural ideas and values, so feminist research seeks to scrutinise the way social and cultural norms create injustices that are experienced differently or uniquely by women and girls. Feminist research theories confound any attempts to categorise feminist theories and methodologies as a single approach to research. Indeed as Ackerley and True (2010) affirm, feminist research does not necessarily require a researcher to identify themselves as a feminist. It does require researchers to engage an ethic which strives to reveal and act upon power dynamics and relationships both within the research subject and within the process by which that subject is researched.

This interest in power dynamics and relationships leads researchers engaged in feminist research not only to examine their own positionality, as ethnographic researchers might, but to also examine their own use of power and how it impacts upon their relationships with the participants and also in the implications of the research findings that emerge. Feminist research does not advocate any particular methods, rather it is the engagement in critical self-reflection and the motivation to use research in order to examine feminist concerns of the use and misuse of power.

Therefore feminist research is interested in studying marginalised and silenced groups within communities in order to question how power manifested within social and cultural practices and institutions lead to their oppression. This leads to the inclusion of feminist research theories in child research both international and global. The emphasis feminist research places on examining power dynamics, and the responsibilities feminist researchers place on themselves to reflect on their role in these dynamics, make feminist research theories congruent with the study of and with children. This approach to child research makes feminist research theories particularly valuable in the study of global child research and in exploring the experiences of children within communities, as demonstrated in the case study below.

CASE STUDY

Return to the case study examined in Chapter 7.

Sircar, O and Dutta, D (2011) Beyond Compassion: Children of Sex Workers in Kolkata's Sonagachi. Childhood. *18 (3): pp 333–349.*

The researchers evoked feminist research principles to interview children from a collective comprising the sons and daughters of sex workers from Kolkata's Songachi region of India. The researchers found the children far from the passive victims of abusive or neglectful mothers portrayed by the media. Their relationships with their mothers were complex and tied into their battles against unscrupulous landlords and government policy aimed at criminalising their mothers' clients.

The study challenged the traditional *compassion-driven* response of *raid, rescue and rehabilitation* that resulted in the forced removal of the children from their mothers. Instead they highlighted the children's counter-response of *resilience, reworking and resistance* as a way to recognise and address their lack of rights, reduced educational opportunities and social stigmatisation. The researchers argued for a need to focus on the opinions of the children central to the issue.

In this case study the researchers described their aims to represent children's '... *own visions of themselves, and not find a definition that will make them easily understood to "mainstream" society. As researchers our attempt is to be ethical witnesses to the emotional and political lives of these children* ...' (Sircar, and Dutta, 2011, p 335).

Critical questions

»   *In your opinion, what power dynamics might the researchers face when attempting to avoid definitions that would make these children* easily understood by mainstream society?

»   *How might they begin to address those challenges?*

»   *Is it possible for researchers to be truly ethical witnesses to the emotional and political lives of children? Justify your answer.*

»   *What are the implications that arise from your answer to that question?*

Children as researchers: the next step

The contemporary view of children as active agents within their own lives and their communities leads children to be seen as more active participants in international and global child research. Children as researchers supports the progression of children's rights as identified in the UNCRC (see Chapter 5) and progresses the viewpoint of children as research participants who can offer *insider perspectives* on children who design, conduct and disseminate research with the support of adults. Children actively engaging as researchers offers them opportunity to participate in issues which impact upon their lived experiences. This not only promotes children's participatory rights but also explores experiences in ways which adults are unable to conceive. Kellet (2005) suggests that child researchers help to address power differentials that exist between adult researchers and child participants while providing a more authentic child perspective on the research subject.

However, children as researchers is not without its challenges, not least is the need to support and train children in conducting research along ethical lines. Indeed while child researchers might address an adult–child power dynamic from adult researchers, it should not be supposed that power dynamics and ethical considerations will be any less when children are researching each other. In the case study below, working in collaboration with children as co-researchers presented the adult researcher and the children with insights into the community that might not otherwise have been achieved.

CASE STUDY

Milstein, D (2010) Children as Co-researchers in Anthropological Narratives in Education. Ethnography and Education. *5 (1): pp 1–15.*

This ethnographic study was conducted in a province of Buenos Aires, Argentina. The researcher worked to build horizontal relationships. She worked with two small groups of children (six and seven in each group) between 10 and 14 years of age as co-researchers in a two-year project. Each group produced booklets to record their data and findings. The children attended a school based within an area with high levels of unemployment and which was struggling with budget cuts, poor teacher authority and breakdowns in school and parent relationships.

Having worked with the children on training in research methods which included interviews and photography, the adult and children were able to research the links between the school and the local community by gathering accounts from adults and children within the community and school. These were then developed into booklets containing the data from drawings, photographs and interviews to create a comprehensive view of social life within the school and the local community and revealed the children's perspective of their experiences in a way the researcher had not fully anticipated at the start of the research. She describes two social worlds, that of the adults and that of the children, arguing that without collaborating with the children as fellow researchers their social world would have remained invisible to her.

Critical questions

» *In your opinion, why did the children acting as co-researchers reveal insights into a social world that could not have been gained without their collaboration?*

» *How might this approach influence child research in the future?*

» *What, in your opinion, are the challenges to this approach?*

» *How could you plan to engage in collaborative research with children as co-researchers within your practice?*

Critical reflections

This chapter has examined the emerging role of research in defining and understanding contemporary childhoods and the issues children face. By examining different methodological approaches it has encouraged you to return to case studies in this book to re-examine them from a methodological perspective.

As new technologies emerge and new challenges and opportunities arise for children and their role in societies, research will invariably need to adapt and change. In doing this the contemporary view of children as active participants within their communities is likely to be a force for shaping how research with children engages with that belief.

The questions below were set at the start of this chapter to compare your answers after having read this chapter.

» *In your opinion, what are the purposes of child research?*

» *What ethical implications might emerge from these purposes?*

» *What role does the researcher play in such research?*

» *How are children viewed in such research?*

» *Reflect upon whether or not your ideas have altered and what this means for your practice and any research you engage in with children.*

Further reading

Ackerly, B and True, J (2010) *Doing Feminist Research in Political and Social Science*. London: Palgrave MacMillan. This book offers a valuable guide and information source for those interested in engaging further with feminist research theories.

Buse, K, Mays, N and Walt, G (2012) *Making Health Policy*. Maidenhead: Open University Press. Chapter 9: Research, Evaluation and Policy provides an in-depth and interesting examination of the relationship between research and policy-making decisions.

Crang, M and Cook, I (2007) *Doing Ethnographies*. London: Sage. This book provides important insights into ethnographic research.

Linsenbard, G (1999) Beauvoir, Ontology, and Women's Human Rights. *Hypatia*. 14 (4): pp 145–162. For a fascinating discussion on the ontological perspectives of human rights.

Penn, H (2005) The Ethics of Intervention, in Penn, H (ed) *Unequal Childhoods*. London: Routledge. For a thought-provoking examination of the ethical challenges in the relationship between minority and majority world nations.

References

Ackerly, B and True, J (2010) *Doing Feminist Research in Political and Social Science*. London: Palgrave MacMillan.

Ariès, P (1962) *Centuries of Childhood: A Social History of Family Life*. New York: Vintage Books.

Bandura, A, Ross, D and Ross, S A (1961) Transmission of Aggression through the Imitation of Aggressive Models. *Journal of Abnormal and Social Psychology*. 63: pp 575–582.

Bell, L and Stevenson, H (2006) *Education Policy: Process, Themes and Impact*. London: Routledge.

Bloom, B, Michaud, C, Montagne, J and Simonsen, L (2006) Priorities for Global Research and Development of Intervention, in Jamison, T, Breman, J, Measham, A, Alleyne, G, Claeson, M, Evans, D, Jha, P, Mills, A and Musgrove, P (eds) *Disease Control Priorities in Developing Countries*, 2nd edn. New York: Oxford University Press.

Buse, K, Mays, N and Walt, G (2012) *Making Health Policy*. Maidenhead: Open University Press.

Clair, R (ed) (2003) *Expressions of Ethnography: Novel Approaches to Qualitative Methods*. New York: State University of New York Press.

Crang, M and Cook, I (2007) *Doing Ethnographies*. London: Sage.

Editorial (1997) International Child Research: Promise and Challenge. *Childhood*. 4: pp 147–150.

ERIC (2014) *Ethical Research Involving Children.* [online] Available at: www.childethics.com (accessed 11 October 2014).

Exenberger, S (2013) The Work of Interpreters in a Cultural Sensitive Environment, in Graham, A, Powell, M, Taylor, N, Anderson, D and Fitzgerald, R (eds) *Ethical Research Involving Children*. Florence: UNICEF Office of Research – Innocenti.

Francis-Chizororo, M (2010) Growing Up without Parents: Socialisation and Gender Relations in Orphaned-Child-Headed Households in Rural Zimbabwe. *Journal of Southern African Studies*. 36 (3): pp 711–727.

Herbert, S (2000) For Ethnography. *Progress in Human Geography*. 24 (4): pp 550–568.

Kellet, M (2005) *Children as Active Researchers: A New Research Paradigm for the 21st Century?* UK: ESRC.

Milstein, D (2010) Children as Co-researchers in Anthropological Narratives in Education. *Ethnography and Education*. 5 (1): pp 1–15.

Owen, R (1991) *A New View of Society and Other Writings*. London: Penguin Classics.

Pols, H (2002) Between the Laboratory and Life: Child Development Research in Toronto, 1919–1956. *History of Psychology*. 5 (2): pp 135–162.

Pryke, M, Rose, G and Whatmore, S (2003) *Using Social Theory: Thinking through Research*. London: The Open University Press.

Sircar, O and Dutta, D (2011) Beyond Compassion: Children of Sex Workers in Kolkata's Sonagachi. *Childhood*. 18 (3): pp 333–349.

UNICEF (2014) *The State of the World's Children 2014: Every Child Counts*. London: United Nations Children's Fund. [online] Available at: www.unicef.org (accessed 10 August 2014).

Waring, M (2012) Finding Your Theoretical Positon, in Arthur, J, Waring, M, Cole, R and Hedges, L (eds) *Research Methods and Methodologies in Education*. London: Sage.

Yardley, A (2011) Children as Experts in Their Own Lives: Reflections on the Principles of Creative Collaboration. *Child Indicators Research*. 4 (2): pp 191–204.

Index